Promises Broken

Child and Adolescent

Edition

DEDICATION

For the
Children - Kids - Students - Teens

Take the first step. Your steps may falter and be uneven and that's ok. Keep going at your pace, when it feels right.
Look up - look for a goal to reach. One of the biggest things to do is find the direction. To make the change, you need to start. I sincerely hope what you find in this book will help you do that.

Best wishes.

Michael

*The jagged edge - either side can be the same;
only the state of mind is different.*

CONTENTS

ACKNOWLEDGMENTS

From

Dr. Mike's Education Blog

http://www.privsec.com/blogs/blog5.php

For Students (and Parents)

**All entries are authored by Dr. Mike. This book
is an edition for kids and adolescents. The items
of general interest are gone. This edition cuts to
the chase. The articles about mental and physical
abuse and survival remain and are reorganized
by topic. Article links are posted in the
Education Blog where they originally appeared.
Just use the search function for the Title and the
original article will appear. URLs mentioned
within an article may cease to work over time as
websites are changed and updated. The CBC,
Foxnews and the Sun are pretty good about
keeping URL's active. Many others are not.**

PLEASE READ

Kids – please read – it may help you
save your life – mental or physical.

Parents – please read – it may help you
help your kids or yourself, or both.

CH 1 : HOPE: YOU ARE SPECIAL!

You are Special! - Child and Parent!

In this day or new age of craziness and worry, the unexpected and multi-vector influences on our children, it may help to know that you the parent are special, and so are your children. Some people would ask, why? Well, simply to survive with your mental and physical health intact is a real challenge and should earn you a "well done, you made it" accolade. However, knowing you made it is usually enough.

Sometimes an event takes place that is so horrific that we cannot grasp it right away. Sometimes an event seems to be at our doorstep. Yet other times, it seems very far away. All of this is in our consciousness and our upbringing, experiences, feelings and perceptions coming into play.

Fear is the catch word these days. Not for ourselves but for our children. We do not have control over our child's environment while they are in school, going to school and coming home. That is the fear part. Things can happen that we have no control or influence over. We trust school administrations and teachers to look out for our kids for us, because we are not there. We have to trust. Sometimes that trust is broken by people bent on destroying anything in their path. Sometimes it is an accident, sudden and fatal.

If you cannot control an action then we try to mitigate the result. As an example, some parents buy bullet-proof backpacks for their kids.

Life for the survivors must go on in a better and more forgiving way than before. Forgiving even yourself, for your thoughts of not being able to protect your child.

We must look ahead and help ourselves and our surviving kids get better. To celebrate life and living and having fun again.

Perhaps this Christmas, we could reflect about what we still have. Not in a material sense, but in a mind, heart and spiritual sense. Our thoughts and memories must be tempered with good, fond, happy reminisces. Heavy sighs will still occur. But your kids NEED to get past their grief, and you, your grief.

Are we showing or demonstrating thanks for what we still have?

We have many rituals and now new ones as well. Honoring our kids at a special time of year. Let's not forget to do that.

Let the healing begin - only you can allow that to happen.

For many it may not be a "Merry" Christmas, but please let it be of fond memories and sharing the load upon your shoulders and hearts.

We need, all of us need, to have a warm, happy thoughtful holiday. I wish you have at least a part of that.

In passing on, our children will not be forgotten. We must live again to honor them fully.

Students, please help your teachers and parents. They need the help and understanding too.

Thank you all...

CH 1 : FOCUS ON THE POSITIVE!

Parents: Focus on the Positive!

Parents, don't focus on the negative aspects of the school work or exam or quiz marks of your son or daughter. They want to hear just as much praise for their good work. Praise, or great positive comments, seem to be missed completely sometimes.

So you give your kid hell for a bad mark and of course do not give your kid a chance to explain it? Do you even acknowledge the good marks? No? Hmmm. Then you wonder why your child is grumpy, in a bad mood, depressed, un-involved, listless, does drugs, swears a lot, wants to beat someone up just to release the tension, et cetera. What is wrong with this picture? Well, you are.

The next time you chastise your child, balance it out with a great compliment. Or heck, just give them a compliment right out of the blue. That moment becomes an incredible WOW moment! Look at their face or eyes when you do - see the wonderful difference.

Have a heart, don't take yourself too seriously. As the old expression goes, no one else does.

Listen well, don't interrupt, understand...

CH 2 : PROMISES BROKEN PART 1

Promises Broken: Part 1 - Dark Side

Promises Broken: Part 1 - Dark Side

Well, how to start... By going back to a beginning...

Questions
Promises

Can you hide the fact that you are not emotionally aging? Yes. If you are 7 years old emotionally, can't people tell that you are not maturing? Nope. What happens? How do you hide it? Why does it happen?

Let's go further back. There was a time when kids were abused emotionally, physically or sexually (which also caused emotional hardship and scarring). It was common. It was not talked about. It was accepted. It was a way of life. Wars broke out; the vulnerable went to war and were killed. That's right, they didn't make it back. The vulnerable today don't go to war. They are confused, questioning, unequipped, naive, gullible, wanting, without goals or direction, not moving on, not growing mentally or emotionally, existing without meaning or purpose. Meaning is important, and without it anyone can be swayed into activities or lifestyles which were never appropriate for that person at all.

Ok, a story then, to help illustrate the points made and to be made.
A young boy of six or seven is manipulated into being a

sex instrument for a male baby-sitter family friend, who never refused a request to babysit. A year and a half after it started, it stopped because the family moved to a different city. The boy by this time had been used every way possible for sex. The boy was damaged goods. The boy did not tell any one. Back then children were to be seen and not heard. The boy was stuck at an emotional level of age seven. In every other way he aged and matured. His attempted suicides at age ten, eleven, twelve, fourteen and sixteen were not understood. His hidden but complete lack of feeling or empathy for anyone or anything else was not understood, or even recognized. It just was. He became a listener by sixteen. After high school he started traveling, anywhere - no destination. By nineteen he was a male prostitute. He believed he didn't deserve any better than to be abused, voluntarily. There was no self-esteem at all by then. He didn't do drugs. He didn't do alcohol. He just did sexual abuse. It is said by some psychologists that a boy who has been sexually abused becomes vulnerable to male-male sexual response. Apparently it is true. So not only is the boy damaged once, but twice. The second damage is for life as well. So the boy is sentenced to a lifetime of hurt and upheaval and broken relationships because of one person. A person who usually gets away with it guilt-free, unknowing, not caring. In this case the person is dead, so the boy, now a man, couldn't go back and face him and ask, why?

There is usually an unwritten promise made to children that they will be looked after and protected. Not all children of course, because not all children are wanted.

So these children are beaten or killed from the time they are in diapers. (A couple of examples of <u>unwanted</u>

http://www.youtube.com/watch?v=M3k70T0Yecc

or <u>beaten</u>

http://www.youtube.com/watch?v=M3k70T0Yecc

Kids on Youtube filmed in a caring way. No emphasis on beatings, more on child response and feeling.) If they live to be in their teens, they are hard and uncaring, just like their parents, if any by then.

The wanted children can be seduced by family or friends or total strangers. And no one knows. And no one talks. What percentages of children are seduced in their early years? Less than one percent? No. More than one percent? Yes. People see a story in the paper about ONE person who was abused. One person. Even if there was a story every day, that would only be a drop in the bucket per year. We are not just talking hundreds of broken kids, but many thousands! Every year!

How can you tell a broken kid? Well, nowadays it is very hard to do. What with dark side interests and drugs, booze and freedom to rein terror upon others, it is hard to tell. Sometimes, if you can talk with a kid alone, then the abused side can come out. It's tough. There has to be a trust. There has to be an interest. Are we seeing a generation of screwed up kids? Yes. Too many bad choices to make, too few good ones. Does anyone care? Well, if people knew the extent of the "problem", probably yes. The news stories are the "tip of the

iceberg". Emergency services know that. News people know that. Child welfare people know that.
Unfortunately for those affected people, they cannot be helped if no one knows, but them. They want, yet don't want, people to know. They live in a catch 22 life with little relief from their reality except for what drugs or alcohol or death can do for them.

For other abused kids who have a relatively normal and loving home life there is going out, ostensibly with friends. There is cutting. There is giving up because they just cannot deal with the FEELINGS any longer. And the family never knows why, unless the child leaves a suicide note. I call it an "ending the pain" note. Some kids don't leave a note. They just decide one day to end it - to leave - to sleep and not wake up, or to watch their life leaving their body and watching themselves die, because they feel they don't deserve to live, or simply don't want to live anymore.

What is it about kids today? Many are like rudder-less ships, not knowing where they are going or how they are getting there. Is it parents? Is it school? Is it their social life? Is it the many distractions available today which can influence them in a negative, or positive, way? This generation has had more input available to them than any other generation in history. Back in the old days it was just about survival, nothing else. Now for many in the world, the only ones who will have a chance to read this, survival is not topmost anymore. Instant gratification is instead. But yet for many populations in other parts of the world where hunger and death are a daily occurrence, survival is all there is, nothing more. So we have a two-world system, trying to exist together. It isn't going to happen peacefully.

Back to our seemingly spoiled first world kids. They really have nothing to whine about, but people (ok kids too!) always look for something to complain about. If the complaint is real, ok. But let's not just imagine it. The problem is, most kids with a real abuse complaint never vocalize it. So we're back to how do we know? How do we tell?

Well, let's look at their eyes. Are they dead eyes? That is, no expression at all? Very few people have dead eyes. They are usually beyond help. Usually, but not always. It is always worth a try. Who knows really, you may be the person who they have been waiting for, who can actually help.

There are those who have a stare that seems to go right through you. There are those who cannot meet your gaze. There are those who try and please you at every turn.

Are rebellion kids damaged goods? Not usually. They like to think they are different, not the "norm" like everyone else. But there really is no "norm" anymore. If children deliberately put themselves in harms' way, there is usually a dark secret reason why. If a child seems to experience, but not react, to pain there is usually a dark secret reason why. If a child stops talking, not completely, just no spontaneous talk any more, or starts talking much more than usual, or avoids contact with adults, or avoids contact with peers, or avoids contact at all, or reads a lot, or stays up very late regularly, or doesn't sleep well, or seems tired most of the time, or spends a lot of time on social network sites that you have probably never heard of, or wears long sleeve shirts or long shorts in the summertime on hot days, or tries to disappear, or is always the quiet obedient one, or has scars but no explanation as to where they came from, or doesn't care, bother, or complain if they eat or not, or are always eating, or say they are too thin or too fat, or give perfectly rehearsed evidence of a mental disorder, or do not have a balanced lifestyle, or go through high school as background students, or don't finish high school at all because they feel they don't "fit in" - which is usually true because they are rebel students, or ??? - We need to ask why.

Now you are beginning to understand that the problem of abused "troubled" youth is much more wide-spread than previously thought. There is no easy answer. But there is always at least one answer.

End of Part 1

Hope is life. There is hope with us all...

CH 2 : PROMISES BROKEN PART 2

Promises Broken: Part 2 - Fix

Promises Broken: Part 2 - Fix

How do we fix the problem? First, there are not enough shrinks in the entire world to deal with the sheer numbers of troubled kids. So, it is up to peers, teachers, relatives, friends, and even strangers sometimes, to lend a hand. Oh, did I mention family? No, because most of the time they don't see anything wrong. They are used to it. They are too close to it.

So let's say we see a child close to us who we believe is a "troubled" youth. How do we approach the subject of "What's wrong?"? The child may not believe that anything is wrong at all. They may be showing the signs and symptoms of some kind of abuse but don't understand that they are abused. It can depend on their age and what they have been told to feel (or not) and whether they believe the abuse is "normal and everyone does it" or not. The big thing is start carefully and explore the topic without saying that you believe there is "something wrong" with them. If they know there is "something wrong", they may not know what it really is. Just that they feel used or dirty or worthless or worse. On the other hand they could feel special, and yet in the back of their mind know that is a different "special". So gaining entrance to their mind and heart is incredibly fragile for both you and the child. By that I mean, if the child opens up because they trust you in some way, or you said the right things, then a very special bond is made that instant. You could easily crush or kill the child emotionally by saying the wrong word or using an indifferent tone and shrug. The child will know. They will probably never trust another person again. If you think you are going to help a child be prepared to hear what could be terrible things to you. Also though, be prepared to hear things which don't seem consequential to you, but they are to the child - or they wouldn't have been said. What is important to a child may be outside your understanding. Accept it. Don't try to understand it. The mistake many friends who intercede make is to try to understand. Unless you too have experienced what they are sharing with you, you will not understand. Don't say "I understand". The child will know instantly that you don't.

The child may think the interested adult won't understand. Give them a chance. You don't know what the adult has already been through and experienced. It may surprise you.

The adult should remember that it is not about you. It is about the child. It may be that the adult and the child are the same age, emotionally. That may explain why a bond can be so easily formed.

The adult can still help the child simply because of the greater life experience already endured.

End of Part 2

Hope is life. There is hope with us all...

CH 2 : PROMISES BROKEN PART 3

Promises Broken: Part 3 - How-to

Promises Broken: Part 3 - How-to

A child's emotional age isn't hidden, it is moderated automatically by learning responses to what is said and done. Emotional age can be faked if necessary, once enough experience is built up. Their private life of emotion is usually all or nothing. They can be very nice and apparently caring. But they never form permanent attachments. They never let go to that degree. They hold back and appear distant at times, which they are more often than not. They never have a long term "normal" life, no matter how much they want one or try to have one.

Sometimes kids want to tell someone but don't know how to start. There is so much hurt. Will they overwhelm the person they chose to listen? Is there enough time? Is there a quiet place where they will not be disturbed, unless they want to be?

So many questions. One answer.
There is always one answer. It may be right or wrong, but one answer. Some factors affecting the answer would be timing, listener, age, location, opportunity, trust, nowhere else to go, accidental meeting, journey, quest, insight, flash of understanding, two plus two, appreciated, recognized, helped, single act, chance. Sometimes it seems preordained. Sometimes it seems like chance will never come.

You stand on a bridge looking at the flowing water below you and it is almost hypnotic, the flow, the sound, the timelessness. You could be there an hour or a minute and you don't know.

You have a sharp knife with a sharp point and you slowly press the point to the vein in your arm and watch it depress the skin, until it breaks through. Then into the vein and blood covers your arm and you are not ready. And you watch. It doesn't seem like that much, and yet blood is everywhere. Well, the true temptation is to let it go on. Just watching. And then, suddenly, it seems sudden at least, a panic appears and the mind, which seemed so much at ease, is now a jumble of thoughts and almost without thinking, a cloth or shirt is pressed to the wound and pressure slows and stops the life-ebbing flow. The wound is bandaged, the mess is cleaned up and no one knows, yet.

Quite often a person who does what I have just described will show and tell a close friend, and swear them to secrecy. But, it's time to tell. Not just anyone. The one who cares and who is calm and reasoned and seasoned. One who can approach the child and listen, and guide. The close friend, your confidant, should bring you to the listener, or bring the listener to you. Trust is established that way. Your confidant will leave. It is time to talk, cry, sob, be held and comforted - and, before it is over, guided in such a positive way as to evoke calm and serenity and anticipation of a changed life and emotional being - and finally, allowing the emotional clock to start again. That may seem like a tall order. But really, it's not. It does require a listener who has time and inclination and dedication to helping others. It is quite often a positive word or a positive belief expressed for another, to another, that makes such a difference. Quite often it isn't going to be the person you thought would listen, but someone you didn't, or even someone you have never met, until now.

End of Part 3

Hope is life. There is hope with us all...

CH 2 : PROMISES BROKEN PART 4

Promises Broken: Part 4 - How-to continued

Promises Broken: Part 4 - How-to continued

What do you do when a person you love gives up? What do you say? How do you act? Why did it happen? How did it happen?

The boy or girl who seems to have given up, look at their eyes. Ask questions and listen to answers, if any. Try to engage the person in some kind of conversation. Try to engage the person with an activity you both can enjoy and like. But even that will wear thin soon enough. New adults (kids who have turned eighteen) are still kids. But we as old adults instantly expect more of them now. And, they are not ready and not yet knowledgeable enough to give you what you want to see. So, tension occurs. As well, the "kids" are trying their wings, and that scares parents. The kids must fly. That's a given. But most parents are scared for their kids, and indeed, for themselves. Parents know the kids must leave and begin to know what it is like to be on their own and making their own decisions. Yes, sometimes the kids falter, and with the knowledge that their parental home is still open for them, they persevere because they have a comforting knowledge which inspires confidence. However, what about the kids who are not coming from a loving and supportive home life? They just want to leave, and usually have already. Street kids who are already "homeless". Fortunately for these kids there are some really good support services today. There wasn't much just twenty years ago. Because of that, there are a number of street people who have lost touch with "normal" people, because they have never known normal, and they hardly feel anymore and believe people are expendable, including themselves. They will knife or punch someone just because they can, and because they don't care. Today's kids have people who are ready, able and willing to help them. The only thing they need to do is ask. That is usually because unless they do, no one knows what they are experiencing. Occasionally kids go through the court system and end up in the hands of strangers who are challenged with helping them. But, for so many kids who have become so desperate as to be involved with the court system, they have "given up". If they are still alive, perhaps all is not lost. For the very, very few it is lost. There is no return, no salvation, no feeling, and no life. For the others, it takes a very dedicated person to reach the kid and help them turn their life around. What they have already experienced, is theirs. No one can take that from them. Anyone can add to it. Help them recognize the people who will hurt them by conning them or by offering them something if they do something in return. Usually the "something" is illegal, and when caught, it is the kid again in trouble, not the person who conned the boy or girl.

End of Part 4

Hope is life. There is hope with us all...

Dr. Mike

CH 3 : YOUTH – DEPRESSION AND BULLYING

Youth - Depression and Bullying

Bullying is not going away. Neither are the effects on a person who is bullied. Depression, and sometimes acting out, could be the usual result. There are many signs a bullied person may exhibit, but it usually takes someone who knows the person to notice the difference between what was "normal" and what has changed. After noticing what has changed, it is time for questions. Unfortunately for parents, most kids don't respond well to questions, with stock answers like "ok", "nothing wrong", "leave me alone", etc. and parents chalking it up to childhood mood swings, especially nearing and into puberty. So quite often a child will tell another of the same, or near same, age but only if asked. The listening child usually will not tell anyone else unless something bad is mentioned. Bullying has been studied to death, as the stories mentioned below illustrate. Recommendations are made. Hardly anyone listens, or takes action on a many, instead of a few, basis. By many I mean the whole school population. It is easy for one or two students to embrace a different way of thinking about bullying. It is much more difficult to get the entire school population to do it. Can it be done? Of course. Creative teachers and creative students are the answer. By creative I mean able to explain and demonstrate the "problem" and present a "solution". Most educators like to give students solutions to problems, or at least help the students find a solution. Most "mental professionals" present recommendations.

19

A recent story from the CBC talks about a new study from the US called, Public health approach to bullying and suicide prevention urged.

http://www.cbc.ca/news/health/story/2013/06/19/bully-school-suicide-prevention.html

Last month mental health experts writing in the Canadian Medical Association Journal about student suicide said, among other things,
Strengthening social connectedness such as supportive home and school environments, boosting individual coping skills and ensuring access to caring adults may pay dividends in both bullying and suicide, they said. They noted poor mental and physical health among victims and perpetrators of bullying and those who experience both.

It is good to see a study reporting what most teachers or parents know. Third party unbiased reporting is excellent and useful.

Here is an excerpt from the article mentioning an interesting, and in my mind, valid point,
As for the question of whether youth who are bullied become depressed or if depressed youth are more likely to be bullied, a Dutch study suggested the answer may be both.
Victims of bullying were much more likely to develop new psychosomatic and psychosocial problems over a school year compared with children who were not bullied, but those with pre-existing depressive symptoms or anxiety were also more likely to be victimized for the

first time.

More is being learned, and like most things, there are a lot of "may" and "could" words in the descriptions of a problem or resolution. No, not resolution - a study instead. Very seldom is there a resolution - just recommendations. Gets everyone off the hook. Mental health is not an exact science, due to the individuality of each person. How we look at mental health today is not the same as just fifty years ago. An example:
People with reasonably serious mental health problems used to be locked away as nut cases in insane asylums. That was mostly because "normal" people didn't want to deal with crazy people nor did they want them on the street. Nowadays however, there are probably as many crazy people on the street as would fill a large city. They, for the most part, are not being treated. So we still have the "may", "should" and "could" in research, studies and stories as the following two items illustrate.

Finally, there is recent noise about sibling bullying. What! This is coming from "professionals" who, it seems to me, just want to make a name for themselves. Well they have - a laughable one.
Siblings always have a rivalry which seems like bullying sometimes, but isn't. On the other hand, I have seen very rare instances of bullying among children in blended families and adoption families.
However, the way the stories are coming out, it seems like ALL siblings are being lumped together as possible bullies.

Here is a "study" published in the Pediatrics journal,

Sibling bullying is under-recognized, study finds.

http://www.foxnews.com/health/2013/06/17/sibling-bullying-is-under-recognized-study-finds/

The CBC reports the same study a bit differently here, Sibling fights compared to school bullying

http://www.cbc.ca/news/health/story/2013/06/17/sibling-bully.html

I hope the "professionals" can do better than that, or is it that they are running out of things to publish... Hmmm

To your healthy mind and body...

CH 3 : IS YOUR PROVINCE/STATE BROKEN

Is your (insert Province/State here) Broken?

In Alberta, the Edmonton Public School Board was trying to push its agenda at the School Board Association annual meeting. Apparently it was about extending protection for gay, etc. youth in schools. Well, the recently passed new School Act will do that quite well. Regulations pursuant to the Act will be forthcoming - with the input of ALL the players, not just the ones with lopsided agendas.

Here are some news stories related to the School Act and the Association decision. Of course, you can't please all of the people all of the time, so a person, the media labeled as an activist, said he didn't agree with the decision. That's ok, it's a free country, and you can disagree, so far.

Alberta school boards reject sex orientation protection policy

http://www.cbc.ca/news/canada/edmonton/story/2012/11/21/edmonton-schools-sex-orientation.html

Trustee apologizes for comments about gay students

http://www.cbc.ca/news/canada/edmonton/story/2012/11/22/edmonton-trustees-gay-alberta.html

Well, on the other hand, perhaps it's not a free country anymore. It seems that if you say anything that upsets even one person, you are in the wrong. Wow. How did we get here?

Too much time on our hands. No wars, famine, sickness or terrorists to have to think about. Spending time for survival is not necessary for almost all of the population. So there is time to spend on bringing down other people - the local and national sport now. From bigots, students, parents, adults in general - engaging in bullying of any nature - well, it's all around us.

We wonder why we cannot get a handle on bullying. Look no further than comments made by so-called activists. I call them fundamentalists. No quarter - no independent thought - absolute belief - nowhere in their heart for the beliefs of another. It's their belief or nothing. Sounds like so many dictatorial leaders over the centuries. And it's right here in North America. We don't have to worry about threats from other countries. The threat is already here - inside most people. There appears to be no realization, no independent thought, just mouthing what others have already said.

Yes, the bullies are back. Well, they never left. The trustee was very politely trying to warn gay kids that they could be the subject of unwanted attention (bullying, words, etc.). The bullies saw to it that he was vilified for his rightful say. The world, and certainly North America, is not at the acceptance level of what some people would like to see. Right now it is a fantasy. Equality of any kind is a fantasy. Just get out into the world and take the rose-colored glasses off. There seem to be a lot of bubble people here. Broken here? Yes.

We are trying to break into the 21st century thinking, studying, teaching, learning and acceptance - with little effect. We are not even close at this time. What will it take? (Well, it won't be the bullying we've seen regarding the news articles mentioned above.)

I hope your learning opportunities are vast, and that you take advantage of all you can do.

(Yes, there is a way...)

CH 3 : UNINTENTIONALLY CRUEL

<u>Kids can be unintentionally cruel</u>

Kids (and adults too) can be cruel without knowing they are. A few words texted to someone about someone else will start it. There is no recall. It can start as a joke or a gentle chiding comment.

Once started, it can snowball to something outside the bounds of the originator's thoughts or mild/joking comment, to something cruel and terrible and long-lasting. The person who is being smeared may not be able to survive the negative comments and attention. No fond memories here.

The good side, positive and encouraging, is intentionally praising or saying a gentle thank you to a person instead. It will be appreciated, honored and remembered for a long time with fond memories. And, you will be a hero... If the exchange is face to face, don't forget to make full eye contact when saying it.

CH 3 : SO MANY BULLIED
SO MANY HURT

Students - so many Bullied - so many Hurt

Bullying is not just what you read in the paper or watch on TV or online. It is something that is ongoing everywhere. Many, many kids endure it and tell no one, and because they do not succeed in killing themselves no one knows.

I believe there is major, or serious, bullying and minor bullying. It can be physical or mental (psychological), or both. Either way, it is torment. Kids have enough on their plate without it. Ongoing torment pushes them over. (Depression, anguish, upset stomach, racing heart rate, sudden despondency, anticipatory anxiety and more)

Here is a Youtube page

http://www.youtube.com/watch?v=ZzQasKcE5ws

of kids who have died, due in part, to major bullying. Look at the side links - there are so many. Be aware that some video links may not be what they seem.

These stories should never have happened. There are people who just want to see others in pain, to cause the pain and torment. What happened to them to want to do that? We don't know. Some do it just because others do it. We do have to put an end to it. More and more and more legislation will not put an end to it, or even slow it down by much. Educate - show the pain and suffering that others have felt without getting sappy. Empathy.

It is said that girls respond very badly to humiliation - girls can become terribly depressed for a long period of time. When they should be enjoying life, they are not. Some who have asked for help didn't get help and they went no further - trust betrayed, not enough left to try again. I say to you, please try again with another person, or the Kids Helpline - they will not turn you down or talk down to you. They will listen.

Please do not become a statistic. Statistics are cold numbers. You are a warm human being, with feelings and hopes and desires. Life is for you!
I KNOW that the pain can be stopped by death. I KNOW is can be lessened to bearable (and less and less pain) by talking with someone. Helping you get through each hour of each day, and night. Kids don't want to feel overwhelmed, ever. If that feeling is ongoing then a major depression sets in, because they care.

I talked with a 16 year old girl less than thirty minutes ago and she advised that she was bullied often and the person she could confide to is her older sister. Her parents don't know and the school staff don't know. Most important, she has someone. If you don't, why not call the Kids Help Phone.

I can be reached by using the Contact feature at this website. The Kids Help Phone is 1-800-668-6868. Their help page about bullying is here.

http://kidshelpphone.ca/Teens/InfoBooth/Bullying.aspx

Please help. Please help us SEE you, RESPOND to you, HELP you.

Parents - every now and then have a critical (as in depth) look at your kids. If there is even the slightest hesitation in response, make time right then to pursue it. There is much more bullying going on than we realize.

Kids - tell someone you trust...Parents or Listener - listen!

CH 3 : ANTI-BULLYING - AGAIN

Anti-bullying - again

Why is it that bullying is not going away? Because no matter what the laws or school rules, or any other punitive response, bullies didn't get the "message".

Education seems to be the common thread. If we can educate in a proper manner, we can reduce bullying, and its effects on the innocent.

Why do some people become victims? By looking at them you wouldn't think they could be the victim. But what goes on in the mind to make them so vulnerable is something we don't know about or understand. We only see the exterior.

We have to look at the people who are bullying-susceptible to tune anti-bullying messages for them. We have to look at a different way to reach the minds of those who may have been bullied so much themselves. They may just be trying to "get even" with the world, since they cannot get even with their own bullies. Bullies hate vulnerable people. They despise them.

Can a bully become a friend? Yes, sometimes. It depends on the victim. What the victim could try is two-way given/earned respect. Some ways to do that is talk to your bully and perhaps he/she will respond in a positive way. Some example openers could be: I want you to fend for me as I cannot do it for myself, I want you to love me, not hate me, I want you to walk with me, not run me down, I want you to hug me, nor knock me down, I want you to be my mentor, not my tormentor, I want you to care about yourself, because I do.

Sometimes there is no reconciliation possible. It doesn't mean the bully cannot be helped to consider their hurtful existence. It just means that you cannot do it. However you are the victim and must be helped. Most of the time, you cannot help yourself, except to end the pain. You, need to talk with someone who will listen, not judge, and keep it as a confidence as a matter of trust.

Don't give up yet...

The following video from the Bully Suicide Project has stories of young people who ended the pain - committed suicide, because they could not take the abuse any longer. They gave up - there were no more choices for them. You are still here. You can be helped if you call out - to someone who will care...

http://www.privsec.com/blogs/blog5.php?blog=5&paged=7

on this page
http://www.privsec.com/blogs/blog5.php/2012/08/12/anti-bullying-again

Want help? Need help? Call help!
800-668-6868 Kids Help Phone

Bullies
Unfortunately, there will always be bullies. Why?
Because of Fetal Alcohol syndrome, among other things

like beatings, burnings, sex toy use, parents who hate them. No one cared about them then or now. These kids are in and out of youth court, youth group homes and eventually as adults, jail. Some people will say we could have helped them. No, not really. Many, many can be helped - if there are enough resources to do it. But for some no, they are really beyond help. There is no humanity left. By their own actions they end up removing themselves from society.

Bad Parents
Look at the recent child deaths due to deliberate neglect, punishment or abuse. Adults who actually hate children, especially their own. It is not a nice world and many people suffer.

Victims
People and organizations try to help. The victims must want help. Must talk. It happened and there is no going back except for some, in their minds, who experienced sudden abuse like rape. They regress to before the sudden abuse and they don't come back because they don't want to come back to pain. But for most victims, there is no going back. Unfortunately there is no going forward emotionally either. That's where help comes in to play. You need help. People are willing, able and want - to help you.

Want help? Need help? Call help!
800-668-6868 Kids Help Phone

CH 3 : CHILD BULLYING FOR REVENGE

Child Bullying for Revenge

Bully the child to get even with the adult.

A parent wrote to me last night and asked whether Alberta has anti-bullying laws. Well yes and no. Nothing officially to do specifically with bullying, although physical bullying could be considered assault and is covered by provincial and criminal code entries. However provincial student anti-bullying legislation, whether coming from other students or adults, is really non-existent at this point. If the new Education Act comes into being, then there will be legislation which expressly deals with bullying. At least to students. Workplace bullying still goes on of course and will continue to do so. The only remedy is to file a human right complaint, which may or may not cover the type or kind of bullying that is taking place. However, if you can't stand up for yourself, you've had it. Of course, some bullying is by whispering and innuendo and that is hard to fight, especially when you don't even know who started it. Sometimes bullying is out of revenge. That is hard to deal with because it won't go away either. Rather than having a third party try to deal with the problem, you may try to confront the bully directly. Then again, maybe not, depending on the circumstances. Here is a Government of Alberta resource to help address workplace bullying.

http://alis.alberta.ca/ep/eps/tips/tips.html?EK=11608

There is student-student anti-bullying legislation is many states and some provinces. I personally have not come across any legislation whatsoever which specifically addresses adult-student bullying.

A recent MacLean's article by the editors called, "Strict anti-bullying laws could actually make matters worse"

http://www2.macleans.ca/2012/03/13/strict-anti-bullying-laws-could-actually-make-matters-worse/

does a nice job or reviewing where we are today after laws and school policies were introduced over the last ten years or so in many areas, especially in the US. It is from a Canadian perspective. It is not encouraging.

So how does all this help when a school child is whisper-bullied by sport authority men to a sport school because they want revenge through the child, to get even with his grandfather? It doesn't help. There is no remedy other than talking with school personnel and getting it straightened out, which works. However the damage is done and revenge complete. There is no justice or law that covers this type of cowardly activity that I'm aware of at this time.

There is a hole in the system, but then there are so many holes in the system. If there were laws for every thing or slight a person could do, we would be drowning in laws and no one would know what to do or not do. Anarchy would reign, in my opinion.

To the child who did no wrong of his own, you are learning that the world is not fair and some people are mean and cowardly. However, you may want to try to right the wrong. Be a better person for it. Think about going to the school and be very, very good at what you do. Be better than they are. You can persevere. You can win. Don't play their game. If you do, they win. Take their rule book and chuck it. You can make your own. Be fair, be honest, and be right (as much as you can be). Once you have a reputation for honesty (which matters so much to so many people), you will win no matter what you do in life. Especially after schooling is finished.

To the parent of this child, persevere too. Be smart about it.
So, what to do in the scenario above? Well, the law is out (because it isn't); however you could explain your side of the story in every newspaper and talk show in the country. There are indeed at least two sides to every story. You are entitled to yours. Just make sure your facts are straight and provable. You don't want to end up on the receiving end of a libel or slander lawsuit. I am saying you could - should you?

Good learning...Good listening...

CH 3 : BULLYING BACKLASH: MORE LAWS BEGET MORE BULLYING

Bullying Backlash: More laws beget more bullying

The article below explains bullying in a way I cannot and it is written by a person with many years of experience and feeling, and who is one of the foremost educators in North America today. His website is an incredible journey with resources for students, parents, educators, school counselors, psychologists or social workers and much more. Be prepared to spend many hours there. It is called, Bullies2Buddies.com. This article is presented here with the author's permission.

Bullying backlash: More laws beget more bullying

By Israel "Izzy" Kalman

Hardly a week goes by before we learn of another tragic case of a child committing suicide because he/she couldn't tolerate being bullied. And the public's response is always the same: we need to pass tougher anti-bullying laws.

Haven't we noticed that children continue suffering despite 12 years of anti-bullying warfare ignited by the Columbine shooting? Year after year children are bombarded with anti-bullying programs, lessons, posters, movies, books, songs and bracelets. They have signed pledges stating they won't engage in bullying and will stand up for victims. They have been informed of the punishments they will receive if they violate anti-bullying policies. They have heard their favorite celebrities rally against bullying.

Yet bullying continues. President Obama declared it to be an epidemic.

The great irony is that the solution is simple and has been known for thousands of years. The solution is not government but wisdom. It is about knowing how to be a victor rather than a victim. When kids acquire this simple wisdom, no one can bully them and any thoughts of committing violence against themselves or others evaporate.

Shouldn't social scientists be considering the possibility that the endless barrage of anti-bullying messages may be making children even more vulnerable and desperate? How should bullied kids feel when they are constantly exposed to the lie of "Bully-Free Zone" posters in school corridors? How can they be indifferent to insults when they are taught that "the sticks and stones slogan is a lie" and that "words can scar them forever"? How can they feel empowered when they are told they are powerless to handle bullying on their own but need the help of everyone around them? How should they feel when they follow the instructions to inform adults on their bullies only to find the hostilities against them intensifying and their peers calling them "snitches"? How can they be optimistic when celebrities declare, "It gets better," but it's only getting worse? Is it any wonder that children despair and take their own lives in growing numbers?

Why is the world's crusade to eradicate bullying failing? It's because it was spawned by panic — panic over school shootings and child suicides committed by victims of bullying. And panic diminishes rational thinking. Panic causes us to willingly relinquish personal freedom and money to the government in return for the hope of safety. And we are willing to excuse all the destruction caused in the process as the price for pursuing that safety.

Foolishly believing that government has the ability to eliminate bullying, we lobbied for tough anti-bullying laws that turn schools into mini-police states. Educators are now required to do double-duty as correctional officers monitoring everything children do and say to each other and punishing them whenever they upset each other. Police states are not happy places for the inmates or the staff.

Anti-bullying laws are actually a Catch-22, for the harder schools try to comply with them, the worse the bullying becomes. They turn children against children, parents against parents, and parents and administrators against each other. And if the schools fail to satisfy both sets of parents, the disgruntled parents invoke anti-bullying laws to sue the school district, wasting humongous sums of money while further escalating hostilities. Tension has reached an unprecedented level in schools courtesy of anti-bullying laws.

If we truly wish to create a peaceful school environment, we need to stop reacting with panic and childishly demanding that the government force bullying out of existence every time we hear of a suicide. Aristotle said, "One thing no government can do, no matter how good it is, is to make its citizens morally virtuous." If laws could force people to be saints, every government would have created Utopia long ago.

People can be excused for never having studied Aristotle. But we all grew up learning the very same lesson from The Wizard of Oz — that government cannot guarantee us complete safety, that the slick politicians in our capitols are no different from circus fortune tellers, and that the character traits required for dealing with adversity are already within us.

No one wants schools to resemble correctional facilities. They are educational institutions created to prepare children for the challenges of life, not to provide them with a false hope of a life without challenges. Bullying goes on in all areas of life. Just as children deserve to be taught the three "R"s, they deserve to be taught the simple wisdom for dealing with bullying. Not only is this wisdom freely available, it will increase academic achievement while preventing future tragedies.

Izzy Kalman is a school psychologist and director of Bullies2Buddies, a program that reduces bullying by teaching kids how to handle it on their own. For more information, visit Bullies2Buddies.com.

From Izzy Kalman in Psychology Today, A Psychological Solution to Bullying,

http://www.psychologytoday.com/blog/psychological-solution-bullying

comes this excellent article called, The True Meaning of the Golden Rule: Love Your Bullies

http://www.psychologytoday.com/blog/psychological-solution-bullying/201002/the-true-meaning-the-golden-rule-love-your-bullies

and this one,
Principle Number Three: the Golden Rule.

http://www.psychologytoday.com/blog/psychological-solution-bullying/201105/principle-number-three-the-golden-rule

Please read and THINK. There is too much react and not enough objective thinking today. Let's "engage" our students, not beat them with lawful scare tactics. A change of thinking and consideration must take place, or we are doomed to make the same error again and again. Please, let's make the change for the better, instead of the convenient.

Good learning...Good teaching...Good listening...

CH 3 : BULLYING – STUDENT AND ADULT

Bullying - Student and Adult - Sorrow and Death in the News

Another death - due to bullying - how many more?

Students don't realize the damage they are causing when bullying. There comes a time when it isn't fun, when it hurts, when the hurt seems to become timeless. The psyche of a teenager is very fragile. An unkind word or action can tip the teen to behaviour which is harmful, or deadly. ***STOP***

Marjorie Raymond, a 15 year old girl from Quebec, committed suicide last week.

Marjorie Raymond hanged herself last week after enduring years of physical and psychological intimidation at her Gaspé region high school.

The CBC article, Dead bullied teen's mom calls for tolerance and peace,

http://www.cbc.ca/news/health/story/2011/12/04/mom-wants-tougher-rules-for-bullies-after-daughter-commits-suicide.html

quotes the mother of Marjorie Raymond, Chantal Larose, *"Larose called her 15-year-old daughter's death "the worst thing that could happen to a mother.'"*. A related article, <u>Bullying blamed for Quebec teen's suicide</u>, helps explain as well.

<u>http://www.cbc.ca/news/canada/montreal/story/2011/11/30/teen-suicide-bullying.html</u>

From the article, *"Marjorie Raymond's mother Chantal Larose says her daughter left a suicide note saying she had been besieged for the last year in their town of Saint-Anne-des-Monts, and couldn't face another day in school."*.

One of the many, many good comments struck home and I quote it here:

at 6:27 AM ET
While this is all very well-intentioned, bullying does not stop at school children: I suffered the worst bullying of my life from a middle-aged co-worker and believe me when I tell you that there is no sympathy and no recourse. Like school teachers and administrators, no one wants to deal with this.
Bullies are miserable insecure people who can only feel good about themselves if they are running down others, or one other. Why this feeble and petty sense of power is fulfilling to them is a mystery to anyone decent, but it is nevertheless a very prevalent feeling among people of all ages. Just look at how some people, young and older, treat shop assistants and serving staff: like chattel to be ordered around and belittled.
Forgive me but I cannot help feeling that some of the people who marched around yesterday have done this as

well and never given it a thought. People were once raised by the Golden Rule of treating others as you would like to be treated; nowadays it's all about me, myself and I and treating others like garbage to fuel one's "self-esteem".
If our children are bullying others to death, they probably learned it at home.

And from Fox News let's not forget that bullying affects everyone. This story is about a boy in New York called, "New York High School Suspends Students After Suicide of Gay Teen", about Jamey Rodemeyer's suicide at age 14 on September 18th.

http://www.foxnews.com/us/2011/12/05/new-york-high-school-suspends-students-after-suicide-gay-teen/?test=latestnews

Kids - students - this must start with you - fix the problem - STOP picking on the "other guy or girl". Fun is fun and joshing around is good and healthy. But know when it becomes mean instead of fun. Not everyone has a thick skin.

When is this going to stop? Only when every kid understands. Sometimes it seems like you need to use a 2x4 just to get their attention. Once you have their attention though, they listen well, and finally understand.

Educate! Education! Legislation is the easy way out, which does NOT work. Education is long-lasting and effective, but labour-intensive.

Let's get with the program Skippy - provincially of

federally sponsored anti-bullying education will go a lot longer and last - in the minds of those who hear it, feel it, know it.

Good learning...Good listening

PS: talking it out does help sometimes :)

CH 3 : BULLYING IN ONTARIO – APPLES AND ORANGES

Bullying in Ontario - Apples and Oranges

Well, according to a CBC report, <u>Anti-bullying bill aims to make Ontario schools safer</u>,

<u>http://www.cbc.ca/news/canada/toronto/story/2011/11/30/toronto-mcguinty-bullying.html</u>

Ontario premier Dalton McGuinty presented an anti-bullying bill on Wednesday. From my perspective, it is a knee-jerk reaction to a high-profile student suicide, which bullying was apparently a contributing factor. There were however, other factors as well.

From the report, *"Students will be able to set up gay-straight clubs to promote tolerance in all public schools in Ontario under new anti-bullying legislation from the Liberal government, Premier Dalton McGuinty said Wednesday."*

Further on in the article, this bold statement, *"We are determined to take the next step to ensure that in our schools we send a very clear, strong and direct message: we will not tolerate bullying of any kind, at any time, for any reason."* Students can be permanently expelled. How this would be done, and what court procedures or process of law, review and appeal, is not explained. (And this legislation is the magic bullet eh!) Wow...

"At least one-in-three Ontario students reports having

been bullied, said Education Minister Laurel Broten.
"We know every single student has seen it, has suffered
some form of it, because the reporting levels are
obviously lower than the level of what's transpiring in
our schools across the province," said Broten." This is
quite a statement. Not believable at all. Reality check
please.

Jamie Hubley, the 15 year old boy who committed
suicide in Ottawa recently, was not only mentioned as
being bullied, leading to his death, but his picture is
included in the article as well. It appears to be trying to
sway people by emotion instead of facts. I am not
minimizing James Hubley's death at all. On the contrary,
it is a very, very sad loss of life. And no youngster
should have to go through despondency so deep and
pervasive that it leads to giving up and accepting death
as the only way out. Indeed, something to look forward
to, to stop the feeling, the thinking, being.

The only thing that comes close to rational common
sense was this paragraph, *"The Progressive*
Conservatives introduced their own anti-bullying bill
Wednesday, which Tory education critic Elizabeth
Witmer said calls for anti-bullying awareness campaigns
at all grade levels."

Towards the end of the articles was this admission, *"A*
lot of bullying takes place off school property, but
McGuinty said the government can't really deal with
that."

"We're not going to pretend that we can somehow reach

out into the broader community, into every nook and cranny, but we'll do our very best when it comes to the physical environment of the school itself."

Unbelievable.

McGuinty even recorded his version of "It Gets Better". Maybe it gets better once a student leaves school or moves to a different school, but... no, it doesn't get better. Nice dream-like cloud though. What is it - why are there so many bubble-people?

I'm just trying to throw a little realism in here. Laws - Laws - Laws. Ok, laws are a fall-back. EDUCATION is the key - for change, understanding, acceptance, awareness - and eventually, by default, a "safer" environment, for all. But education takes money, people and time. Perhaps it's just easier to pass a law instead.

Do I sound a bit jaded and disillusioned? Well ok, you've got me. I've seen this before and the results are nil. Education works. Education is hard work. Education requires a change in attitude. Who is going to sponsor this anti-bullying education initiative? Who will see it through?

Darn, is there no one who will guide and manage this task? We're not talking sex-ed here. But we are talking about something just as fundamental. Respect for each other.

Simplistic isn't it? Too much so? I think not. Easy to say - hard to do. Respect is Attitude. Attitude is learned from the cradle on up. It is the biggest challenge of all = to change something, a belief, so ingrained, so deep, that we feel it is a very part of us - not to be challenged or questioned in any way. I believe our (universal) challenge is to help ourselves and those we help along the way, to consider others, as we do ourselves. It is not easy, and not completely doable in our lifetime. But if we don't start now, nothing will change at all, and hate and dislike will still rule the lives of so many, and pain and sorrow will still be rampant - as it still is today.

It could be a better world for our kids - a little bit at a time - but better in some small way is better than nothing at all.

Good learning...Good teaching

PS: There is Point Of View question on the CBC page which asks the question, "Should bullying be considered a hate crime?" Just think about it for a few minutes. Some bullying, a very small fraction, could be considered hate-inspired. But almost all the rest is not. It is usually to make fun of, not hate. Bullying "crimes" make the news. So out of hundreds of thousands of students in Canada, how many are bullied on a daily basis, or bullied so much it makes the news? Newsworthy, maybe one a week - or a month? Of course, what we call bullying today does take place. But a "hate crime"? No, I think not. If it becomes a "hate" crime, then anything we do or say, no matter how innocuous, could be considered a "hate" crime, to someone.

What would be good is a definition of the word "bully",

in the context of school or students that would be the same across the country. At this time in history the definition changes between school boards in the same city.

CH 3 : BULLYING – WHAT ARE WE DOING ABOUT IT?

<u>Bullying - What are we doing about it?</u>

Bullying is still rampant in school, especially high school. By high school, kids have refined bullying in ways not imagined by their parents. Which is why their parents say, "no way!", when their son or daughter is caught and the principal is having the conversation with the parent. Back in the old days, BD (Before Digital), it was easy to spot and deal with most bullying incidents. Now it is a much different story.

More and more resources are available to help stop bullying. But the tide has not turned, and in my opinion, is nowhere near doing so. An article appeared in the Edmonton Journal today called, "<u>Stop the bullying? If only there was a program that works</u>" (dead link). The article originated with the Regina Leader-Post. Here is an excerpt:

Perhaps, there is a school anti-bullying program somewhere that works. If so, Rod Dolmage would love to see the evidence.

The University of Regina education professor has been quoted in the past as saying school anti-bullying programs don't work. Not so, this veteran academic, actually says, "I can't find any evidence that they work."

Dolmage has a theory as to why anti-bullying programs don't work. Read about it all by going to the link above.

There is a link from the article above to a site called, http://www.stopabully.ca/. One of the articles at the site, found on this hard-to-find teacher resource page,

http://stopabully.ca/resources/teacher-bullying-resources

is a very good, realistic and straight-forward story about high school bullying called, Bullying - A Teacher's Perspective, by a high school teacher who sees it every day.

http://stopabully.ca/resources/teacher-bullying-resources/85

Going back to the title question, what are we doing about it, a lot of things. School assemblies, videos, guest speakers, rules, regulations, web sites like stop-a-bully (above), b-free.ca from Alberta Government, bullying.org created by a father and teacher Bill Belsey, and on and on. These are excellent ways to spread the message and are terrific resources.

Good intentions-1, Results-0.

Every now and then a story will appear about one of the approximately 300 kids who commit suicide each year in Canada, and bullying will be attributed as a major factor leading to the death of the student.

Adults have taken the lead and got the counter-bullying movement going. It's time for the kids to take the lead. And that, folks, we can help make happen!

Good learning... Good teaching...

CH 3 : PHYSICAL VIOLENCE – BULLY – ATTITUDE CORRECTION

Physical Violence - Bully - Attitude Correction

Is the school bully waiting for you?

The following commentary is what I did as a kid in high school. I include it as a short essay in this blog because it worked for me.

If you are blind-sided by a bully, wait. You need to be in full control of yourself before confronting the bully. When YOU are ready (on your terms), try talking with the bully face to face, no more than four feet apart. Look the bully straight in the eyes and, very quietly and slowly, say, "don't ever attack me again". Don't waver. Don't make threats. Don't back off. Don't talk. Don't break the stare. Don't answer the usual "or what!". Wait a few seconds and move one step closer. Hands and arms in a neutral position. Summon every bit of energy in your mind and body and while staring repeat, "don't ever attack me again" - in a very controlled low voice, but with a lot of umph behind it. (As if you were ordering someone 30 feet away to comply.) Do not shout! Say it low in volume, quietly, slowly (each syllable pronounced) - and with umph (tense up your tummy but take a deep breath first). Practice using a full mirror at home. If the bully hasn't backed off by then (99% will), then move one step closer and repeat the above. Keep looking at the bully's eyes. You may see uncertainty or a silent 'what is he doing?'. One of three possibilities will develop. The bully will back off, or will strike, or will apologize and be your friend. Be prepared for the strike. Make sure there are witnesses. Now, for me there was no strike. However if there is a strike, you could get hurt. I personally was prepared for hurt and pain. Some people cannot deal with pain, or the possibility of being punched or kicked. But then the bully has probably already done that, and the threat of more keeps you in a locker of mental anguish.

Your mileage may vary. Don't forget, this is what worked for me. Hopefully it would work for you if you try it, however it may not.

Am I saying you should try it if need be? No, but you may wish to consider it as an option you didn't have before. It was an option for me. There are no guarantees whatsoever, because it all boils down to YOU.

Don't have the victim attitude. Instead, have a survivor attitude!

Good learning...Good Listening...

CH 3 : CYBERBULLY VICTIMS – HEALTH PROBLEMS?

Cyberbully victims - Health Problems?

Perhaps there will be enough money in the Alberta Education budget to address one of the fastest growing threats to students today: cyberbullying.

Here is a news article from the CBC

http://www.cbc.ca/technology/story/2010/07/05/cyberbu llying-teens-health.html

with more detail.

An excerpt from the article states, "In 2008, a study commissioned by the Canadian Teachers' Federation suggested that 34 per cent of Canadians surveyed knew of students in their community who had been targeted by cyberbullying in the past year, and almost one in 10 knew someone close to them who had been cyberbullied.".

I would hope that a student experiencing this form of bullying would tell their parents, and the school counselor.

A student telling a friend is great and should be done, but a parent or counselor may be able to actually do something about it.

Good teaching... Good learning...

CH 3 : ANTI-BULLYING LEGISLATION IN ALBERTA

Anti-Bullying Legislation in Alberta

Anti-bullying legislation in Alberta doesn't exist, yet.

MLA Heather Forsyth, introduced Bill 206 which is proposed legislation which has passed first reading in the house. It is said to entail banning weapons and drug items in school or on school properties or at school activities. Here is more, an excerpt from an Edmonton Journal article called, Anti-bullying initiative panned, "*The proposed legislation features a clause which would legally ban bullying, both in schools and online—even if students aren't using school computers to target others.*"

I like it. But apparently some others don't. Near the end of the article a person is quoted as saying, "*If the government is committed to combating bullying and violence, it should be focusing on education programs*". You know, education programs have been going for several years now. And guess what, bullying still occurs! Knowing there is a consequence to bullying should dampen activities related to bullying. So I'm for it and I'll bet most parents are too.

Some academics say it will create more paperwork. Well, what about the student being bullied? Do the paperwork, counsel the student and get the school police liaison officer involved. Don't forget to press charges against the bullies. If you don't, they will just keep doing it - because they got away with it. Don't let that happen.

Police in Alberta are now charging bullying students with assault. Schools are suspending, and considering expelling, students for assaulting other students. Good. It's time for the slap on the wrist to stop and punishment to get serious.

We are lucky here though. Schools have an anti-bullying message for all students at the beginning of the school year and anti-bullying messages are visible through the use of posters and talks during the school year. Not all provinces or states are so lucky. Here is just one article,

http://www.news.com.au/story/0,27574,26100571-421,00.html

from Australia, which show a greater bullying problem there. A quote, "*The NSW Government yesterday acknowledged cyber bullying was spiraling out of control by calling a crisis conference of experts to debate ways of making children safer. Child psychologists, academics and teachers would be invited to the conference in early November*".

In the US, anti-bullying laws have been passed in many states since 2001. Here is an actual study and breakdown for 18 states as a PDF file (add the .pdf extension when saving it).

http://gwired.gwu.edu/hamfish/merlin-cgi/p/downloadFile/d/16896/n/off/other/1/name/GreeneandRoss5237Paperpdf/

At least our government is trying to do something about it here in Alberta. There has been a lot of reaction in the past, but now is the time for pro-action.

CH 3 : BULLIES AND VICTIMS – HOW NOT TO BE A VICTIM

<u>Bullies and Victims - How not to be a Victim</u>

How do we start this topic. There is no beginning and there is no end. So, I'll start somewhere in the middle.

The school year is starting again and so are the bullies. Whether showing off or acting out, there is no room for it. However, it is a fact of school life. How you deal with it is the subject of this post.

I don't normally link to web pages that have language which includes swear words. However, the following post is so powerful about being bullied that I include it. Please be warned.
Here is an article called, <u>I had Death Threats in High School</u>, by Chris Pirillo, which is about being bullied in high school. Read the comments too.

<u>http://chris.pirillo.com/i-had-death-threats-in-high-school/</u>

Here is another entry from a different perspective called, <u>What Is Worse - a Sexual Predator or a Bully?</u>

<u>http://chris.pirillo.com/what-is-worse-a-sexual-predator-or-a-bully/</u>

Here is a quote from that article, "*Are you being bullied? Don't just sit there and take it - report it! Nobody will think you are a wimp or a baby. Go to your parents, a teacher, your boss, or an adult you trust that would do the right thing. If you know of someone who is being bullied, don't assume that it's all in good fun or the person can take care of themselves. You just might be wrong.".*

Here is a link to a very good page from Edmonton Mixed Martial Arts called, How To Defeat A Bully.

http://www.edmontonmixedmartialarts.ca/index.cfm?page=14

The following excerpt is slightly out of context because you need to see the rest of the article for its fit. However, how not to become a victim is the premise in the article and this is just one item mentioned.

"What is the first line of defence? Self-Confidence! Here's why. Bullies choose their victims much like a criminal would choose their victim; they go for the easy and obvious target. So if your child looks like a kid who will get bullied, guess what, they're going to get bullied. On the other hand if your child radiates self-confidence they are less likely to be a victim, it's almost that simple!" There is more of course so please have a read of the article.

Whatever you do, don't get mad or angry, become afraid or ignore it. You lose control of the situation if you do. Being afraid usually means pain or abuse, whether physical or mental trauma, has happened before. The victim didn't know how to deal with it. People don't stop learning. Learn to overcome fear, through training by way of contact sports, strength training, martial arts or other training which teaches discipline, movement and self-confidence. **Gaining self-confidence through whatever means you choose, is the key to not being a victim.**

There are no guarantees of course, because it all boils down to YOU. Don't have the victim attitude. Instead, have a survivor attitude.

Personal references (in this book):
Dealing with some aspects of Bullying in School

http://www.privsec.com/blogs/blog5.php/2009/07/03/dealing-with-some-aspects-of-bullying

Don't be the Victim

http://www.privsec.com/blogs/blog5.php/2009/07/03/don-t-be-the-victim

Fight training for Students

http://www.privsec.com/blogs/blog5.php/2009/07/02/fight-training-for-school

I hope you have a great and safe school year.

Learning counts...

CH 3 : DEALING WITH SOME ASPECTS OF BULLYING IN SCHOOL

Dealing with some aspects of Bullying in School

Bullying can affect kids from kindergarten through high school and beyond. Because of the amount of supervision, bullying in kindergarten to the end of elementary school is usually nipped in the bud. However middle school (or junior high) is usually a breeding ground for those who really like to pick on others. High school can be really bad for some students as bullies are bigger or stronger and may have picked up some bad habits on the street or from their parents.

We know that bullying is not tolerated at school, but that does not stop bullying at all. It just means that bullies pick their time more thoughtfully. Make it look like an accident. Whisper instead of shout. Evil look or gestures. Swarm. Most bullies are cowards and if picking on a same size person or a person who shows no fear, they usually do it in a pack. Gives them courage. But one on one, no - that's when fear makes its appearance. However, some bullies think they can take on anyone. It's just that they haven't learned that there is always someone who is quieter, smarter, faster, stronger, or more competent.

There are a lot of resources available for parents and teens about bullying and three are referenced below.

How to not be a bullying victim? Learn how not to be a victim, which will be covered in another blog entry.

From KidsHealth, we have this article called, Dealing with Bullies. This is a great website with lots of info for kids, teens and parents.

http://kidshealth.org/kid/grow/school_stuff/bullies.html

Also from KidsHealth there is this article called, What Kids say about Bullying.

http://kidshealth.org/kid/feeling/school/poll_bullying.html

From the US Dept of Education there is this good article called, Friendships—Helping Your Child Through Early Adolescence, which would help parents and teens avoid situations where parents are not aware of bullying with their children.

http://www.ed.gov/parents/academic/help/adolescence/part9.html

There is no place for bullies. Some respond to guidance and some don't. The ones who don't usually end up in walkaway homes because they are unmanageable. They are most vulnerable to a life behind bars as well. So, if you can, try to talk with those who are on the bullying path. It may not be too late to help them.

Some website resources advise that fighting back is not the answer as it is violence. Well, I think people should learn to defend themselves.

Dr. Mike

CH 4 : CHILDHOOD SEXUAL ABUSE

Childhood Sexual Abuse

This web page nails it - all on one page.

There are many books written on the subject expanding the points made here but it all boils down to these essentials, which are, unfortunately, all too true.

Adult Survivors of Childhood Sexual Abuse

http://rainn.org/get-info/effects-of-sexual-assault/adult-survivors-of-childhood-sexual-abuse

A couple of brief excerpts:

While each individual's experiences and reactions are unique, there are some responses to child sexual abuse that are common to many survivors...

While each individual's experiences and reactions are unique, there are some responses to child sexual abuse that are common to many survivors...

Please see the website for the complete article.

CH 4 : DEAD EYES

I've Seen the Dead Eyes

I've seen the dead eyes of kids and adults who have been killed emotionally. Their physical person is alive, existing. But emotionally - they are dead.

How did it happen? Well, for many very young girls and boys, being raped and not getting the mental help needed to overcome the incredible emotional damage. For others, the same emotional damage over and over again. Sometimes it is physical damage before birth. For others, losing all hope. No hope.

Can you survive without hope? Yes, without feeling. You could hurt or kill someone and not feel a thing, not care at all. It would be like an object which has no meaning to you.

Meaning - there isn't any. Existence only.

People with dead eyes are very few and far between. Kids with dead eyes are heart-breaking.

Caregivers - parents - get help for the kids before it is too late and they die inside.

Kids - you need help - you know you do - call the Help Phone 1-800-668-6868.

To life - To meaning - To feeling...!

CH 4 : ABUSE: SADD

shock anger depression disbelief

You are a kid and have been used and just found out.

First

shock anger depression disbelief - what to do - humiliation

deep despair

pain in your stomach - stabbed in the back

you feel (know) that no one cares

words to them - feelings for you

you - them

senseless

Perpetrators play too many video games - no connection with pain and suffering - at all. Think before talking - think about the possible outcome.

What are the words that can destroy you? Whether you are a girl or boy it only takes one sentence.
One sentence - 20 seconds - a life destroyed

No one is as tough as they, or you, believe.

Most victims are from middle-class families and have been protected as much as possible. They do not know what to do, or how to act. They are lost and afraid.

Second

The Victim
You are hurt. You are as a wounded animal. Other animals will feel it, know it, and hunt you down, play with you and drive you to panic. Then they attack. It was just teasing before. When the attack comes you are defenseless because they have worn you down.
You must have trusted support to survive. Or, you must have no more animals preying on you.
You must not be the victim any longer. Healing can then begin - and it takes time.

You know your death can end the pain - the thoughts in your head. But it is a little too permanent. You feel that the next day could be a lot better (because you still have HOPE!). Get just one person as your true friend and start the fight back. Your reputation? Respect will help you gain it back. Do a speech at a school assembly. Let everyone know how bad it feels and what you are going through. Look your peers in the eyes - show fear no more, show compassion instead. Why? I have seen young teens recover from strong hurt (spent a little time in hospital getting their head back on straight) and go into a very hard shell of not showing any emotion at all. Ever. They are nice and polite. They have purpose and carry out plans. They do not allow themselves to feel. You need to find the middle ground again. To feel is good. To feel bad is not good, but usually the good far out-weighs the bad.

So there is no easy answer. Suicide is very quick and final. Living to win again will take more time and the long term enjoyment and happiness will be so good. It can be done. Will the memories go away? No, but the memories will dull. They won't have the impact you feel right now. You will learn, hopefully, a coping strategy for dealing with remembering what you don't want to dwell upon. One person I know well says to himself, " no, not anymore", and fills his mind with not that and switching to a good experience and memory. It works pretty well all the time for him.

My only wish for all the hurt children is that they recover, become strong again, can smile again and can look you in the eyes.

CH 4 : ABUSE: WHY ALWAYS 7 YEARS OLD?

Perhaps a Clue? - Why Always 7 Years Old?

We have talked about a traumatic event which doesn't allow you to go beyond the mental age you were when it occurred. Here is a story about brain research which may shed some light on **why**.

A quote from the CBC article states, "*Another curious question has emerged from Lanius' research. Why does the default mode network appear fractured in people who have experienced childhood trauma? Using brain imaging technology, she has shown that adults who experienced childhood abuse have a default mode network pattern that resembles the pattern of a seven-year-old child.*"

Here is the article from the CBC - Seeking seat of consciousness in dark side of brain

http://www.cbc.ca/news/health/story/2013/01/02/health-inside-your-brain-dark-side.html

"*Researchers also hypothesize that damage to the default mode network might explain other mental illnesses.*"

This may help quite a bit as far as treatment goes. PTSD (post-traumatic stress disorder) is huge and so many suffer because of it. The article is definitely worth a read. It may give some people hope.

Perhaps, with understanding, some people can be helped. I hope so. I've come across so many who are stuck at a young age regarding feelings, depression, anger, desire, hope, pleasing and fatality. Some folks can hide it quite well. However their way of coping quite often gives it away.

Learn - Respond - Hope...

CH 4 : THE AFTERMATH: CHILD SEXUAL ASSULT

The Aftermath: Child Sexual Assault

The aftermath after a child (or teen) is sexually assaulted is finally expressed by four people, now adults, who went public, even though they knew there would be a lot of publicity. The court case of Graham James who, over the years assaulted several boys in a Canadian hockey league as a coach, has made headlines both in Canada and the United States.

Theoren Fleury, Sheldon Kennedy, Todd Holt and Greg Gilhooly were involved as victims during their teens. Holt broke down while reading his victim impact statement in court on February 22nd in Winnipeg.

Really, there is no rest for sexual assault victims. There is no lessening of the pain. The experience screws the victim up for the rest of their life. They can learn to deal with it, but the memory, and more important, the feeling, didn't go away. A good, experienced helper/listener can make a big difference helping to bring the victim back on track, for the most part. The problem was, there were no listeners then. No one to help. Today there is. For your own mental, emotional and spiritual health and sanity, get started now. *Who do you tell? The number one choice is a "friend". The number two choice is "no one".* Please don't make the second choice.

Please see the two newspaper articles for more. One

article from the Edmonton Journal

http://www.edmontonjournal.com/news/show+leniency+
Theo+Fleury+says+Graham+James+awaits+sentence/61
90572/story.html

and the other is from CBC Edmonton.

http://www.cbc.ca/news/canada/edmonton/story/2012/02
/21/mb-graham-james-sentencing-hearing.html

The victims are STILL suffering!

Be careful out there. Remember, you can talk with
someone these days! It's not like it was 10 or 20 or 30
years ago. You can tell someone today!

It is after the fact, isn't it? It has already happened to
you. You feel like crap. There are many more words to
describe the feeling but enough to say you do not feel
good about yourself anymore.

Call for help now. Most police forces have a victim
services unit. If that scares you, then call a specialized
help line, like the Kids Help Phone 1-800-668-6868.
Waiting only makes it worse.

http://www.kidshelpphone.ca/

Please see this previous post, called "Learning: after
Child Sexual Assault"

http://www.privsec.com/blogs/blog5.php/2012/01/20/lea
rning-after-child-sexual-assault

and this one called, "Sadness: I Don't Want to be Sad Anymore" as well.

http://www.privsec.com/blogs/blog5.php/2012/02/21/sadness-i-don-t-want-to-be-sad-anymore

Watch out - for yourself - and for others...

*_ Said by Faron Gogo, the Youth Engagement Coordinator for Youth Net in Ontario, to a group of students during a stop bullying presentation._

CH 4 : LEARNING: AFTER CHILD SEXUAL ASSULT

Learning: after Child Sexual Assault

This story of a male nurse assaulting two boys, aged 11 and 13 is representative of what is happening to children day after day after day.

http://www.cbc.ca/news/canada/calgary/story/2012/01/1 3/calgary-sex-assualt-male-nurse-alberta.html

This blog entry is not about the nurse, it is about the boys, and all children who are sexually assaulted, raped; during what is supposed to be their age of innocence. The father of the 13 year old boy is quoted as saying that, "...his son has been scarred for life".
A Calgary Police official is quoted as saying, "[Both victims] are certainly shaken by what has happened and certainly experienced something that no child should ever endure...".

NOT OK!

The article is written as if the kids are things, objects. Every article I have read is the same. See this article about the assault of 2 boys aged 7 and 8 at the time.

http://www.cbc.ca/news/canada/edmonton/story/2012/01 /13/edmonton-castillo-cortes-defence.html

The lengths which one father took after his son was kidnapped and assaulted are documented in a video which shows the father killing the abductor. A Google search for "Father of Kidnapped Son gets Revenge" will show a YouTube link to the video.

But - all of this is still not about the boys or girls who are now emotionally scarred.

About the only thing we know is that each child survived, physically. Emotionally and mentally for some, dead. Look at the eyes. Existing without living. For other kids who have not died in their minds and hearts, they get trapped at the age that the assault took place. They mature but emotionally don't move on, cannot move on. For a few, they can move on, after a lot of help from the right people at the right time.

Some of the victims stop caring - about anything. They exist, acknowledge others, appear "normal" and do not care. Some victims turn to hurting themselves by starving or cutting or other harmful activity that will focus their pain to achieve relief, however temporary. Some victims turn to drugs, alcohol or sleeping pills to help dull and blur the emotional pain. Some victims just fake it and hurt all their lives, allowing no one to see them as they really are - in pain. Relationships are usually not deep enough to last. Some victims kill themselves - they simply don't want to feel the pain for another day, another hour, another minute. This can evoke an incredible sadness, leading others to do the same, or eventually exhibit some of the same behaviors of the original victimized child. The death of this child is needless and shatters the lives of all around who knew the child. Loss and sorrow, deep and pervasive, will haunt the survivors of this child.

The child - the boy or girl - what about them now? Why didn't they call for help, or maybe they did but it was not acknowledged. We won't know. We will just know that another child died - of hurt and pain that they could not deal with - and perhaps their death could have been prevented. Help must be now, not tomorrow or next week, or when convenient for others.

So, what about all of these victims? No - they are just kids - children! Remember that - innocent children!

Oh right, we never hear about them again. Buried. Forgotten. Not newsworthy.
Are there people and agencies that can help? You bet! But perhaps we need to become aware of the terrible consequences of what has happened to the victimized kids and their families. Perhaps this can be done through a series of articles in local newspapers. Then, maybe, fewer kids will be victimized.

How does all of this relate to Learning? Well, learning can actually stop completely. Learning can taper off due to lack of interest, not wanting to be there, not important anymore, no one else understands, ashamed to tell but want to, not innocent anymore while class-mates are, and on and on.
Some teachers can catch on, some cannot. Having your daughter or son molested at an early age is not usually something that is passed along, to anyone outside the immediate family.
How to cope? For the child, expert help is really needed. For the teacher, guidance is needed. For the father or mother, guidance and help is needed. What is being said

here is that "help" is "needed". Not just a nicety, but actually needed, sometimes desperately needed. Helping your child to learn to cope is big.

Are there any easy answers or solutions? No.

Is the sexually assaulted boy or girl scarred for life? Yes.

Do we know what "scarred for life" means? It means all the behaviors mentioned above and much more. Withdrawal is a really big (in your face) symptom, shared by many survivors of sexual assault. Emotional and relational withdrawal. Another common symptom is, being very obedient or not obedient at all. There are as many signs as there are emotionally scarred children. But there are similar behavioral characteristics between many children who suffered sexual exploitation or assault.

We can normally fix something once we understand it. But there is no fix so far. Perhaps we really don't understand it. We see the after-effects, yes. We haven't been able to stem the tide.

The kids need help from their peers who have also suffered the same way or with similar feelings and who have accepted the fact and healed as much as possible.

Has every helper experienced everything? No. So can they say "I understand"? No, not always. They can say, "Please talk to me, I will listen".

From the pages of Critical Incident Stress (CIS) debriefings and Post Traumatic Stress Disorder counseling sessions, we know that it is very helpful if the peers (of any age) have experienced the same job stressors or avocation stressors as the person who needs help.

So for children, even though the age difference between "helper" and child may be great, it should not be significant if the "helper" has experienced some of the same "feelings" or "experiences" as the child in emotional turmoil who needs help.

Sometimes the parents need more help than the child. Sometimes the parents make it worse for the child. For the child, the shock is over. For the parent it is just beginning - and the parent will experience all the symptoms of shock. But much more as well. Guilt is a big one. Guilt - not being able to protect their own child - son or daughter. Knowing that their son or daughter is damaged. There is no going back. No, I wish it was different...

So many parents cry themselves to sleep because of it - the CIS, the eyes of their child, the emotional ups and downs, the courts, the police, hospital examinations, family, friends, and the accused.

The child with wet eyes going to sleep exhausted, and medicated.

The whole family - lives changed forever - trying. Don't give up! Please don't give up. Your child is counting on you. You are the only thing between sanity and death. Death of mind, body or spirit. Parents, family, don't give up. Keep believing, keep hoping - and pass your belief and hope to your child!

Your child - your son or daughter - needs you so desperately. Your child needs to "believe" that you don't dislike them, that it wasn't their fault, that they are not guilty of "something", that they are worth more than before because they survived, that they matter, that they are good, that they deserve to live and be ok, that they are not marked, that they are not different now (more life "experience" yes, but still the same child they were before), that they are still loved, that they are still wanted.....

Parents - support your child! Your child cannot support you at this time!

Child - boy or girl - this is to you.

In some ways you are not a child anymore, but just in some ways. I am not minimizing what happened. No, it happened, it matters, it will be remembered. BUT, where you need help is to remember without re-living it. Whoa - how is that?

There, is an answer. It is not the cure-all. It is the start of healing. You must start - to be yourself again. Can you be yourself again? Yes, with a bit of a different outlook than you had before. Sometimes you will just gaze off into the distance, and then be back to your surroundings in an instant. Will you be different? Yes, by being aware of some things that you were not aware of before. It is another day now and what you experienced is very personal and both physical and emotional. Can you forget it? No, but over time you won't have to re-live it. For your survival, you need to get through the next few weeks. There are people who love you and care whether you live or die. Remember that when you're down. Find a hug-person in your family. That is, one who will give you a big hug, whenever you want or need it, without question or even saying anything. You need it, and believe it or not, they need it too.

What did you lose? A part of childhood, innocence and trust. Trusting those around you, and strangers, will affect you for a long time. You were left in the care and trust of another. Your parents trusted another. How can you trust another person again? You won't for a while. The only reason you "trust" your family is because you know them so well. But even at that it is hard. Words and phrases said aloud have new meaning. Confusion reigns. It will take time to even out your emotions and trust another, even a little bit, again. For your own health, you must try. Don't close up completely. How can anyone help you if you do?

Do you sleep with the light on? Do you sleep with the door closed and locked? Do you jump when you hear or feel an unexpected sound (not loud, just unexpected)? How is your self-confidence? Do you have feelings of guilt? Do you have feelings of resentment? Do you have feelings of anger? If someone says your name, how do you respond? If someone is looking at you, what do you do or say or feel? Do you sigh a lot? Are you sad most of the time? Do you feel lonely? Do you feel hopeless? Do you "feel" at all anymore? Do you spend a lot of time in your room, perhaps pretending to be reading a book? Do you go for walks alone? Do you "chill" with anyone? Do you clench your fists a lot? Are you getting pain in each side of your neck?

You need help. Will you take help if it is offered?

If help is not offered, call for help. A total stranger will answer. Try not to be afraid. Talk - explain why you are calling. That will be one of the hardest things you ever do. Let the person who answers the phone help you. You have control. Please let them help you, as much as you can accept. If you feel you need to talk with someone again, call again.
Kids Help Phone 1-800-668-6868

My sincerest wish is that you survive, and can smile a great smile again.

Added 12-02-01 - I found this and must share it with you, with my emphasis. I found it here.

http://robert-hengst.com/ChildAbuse/ChildAbuse.html

You need help. Therapy is key, but there has to be "an end." Abuse happened in time and there should also be a resolution in time. There will be lasting affects and things that become an intrinsic part of who you are, but abuse and the pain of it should not be a lifetime sentence. Find somebody that can give you help with a discernable "end." ...

CH 4 : THE HIGH SCHOOL KIDS
UNDER THE RADAR

The High School Kids under the Radar

After watching my son in his first year of high school, I have learned about some kids in high school who are troubled teens and cope by hanging out with like-minded kids and miss an inordinate amount of classes. They have found high school to be more onerous that expected and don't have good coping skills. Almost always, their home life is not supportive. These kids are consistently missing classes. Some indicate a desire to go to a different, or alternative, school where there is much less structure. They also feel out of place in their current school. Some of these kids are damaged in one way or another. Many have suffered physical or emotional abuse. Emotional abuse is much more common. They don't know what to do and most don't ask for help, or indeed, don't know how to ask for help.

Many of these kids don't want to stay at home as there is no perceived support there. They begin to stay over at friend's houses for longer than one night at a time.

This kid underground is hard to spot. The kids are not on the street. They move from one house to another, often under the guise of staying overnight and they will tell the host parents that it is ok with their own parents, which usually is not true. The host parents have their own troubles with their own kids and in trying to win them over, accept the extended stay of their kid's friends. One kid I'm aware of is 18 and is about 14-15 emotionally and hangs out with the troubled 14-15 year old kids because that is where his head is at this time. That is where his comfort level is. Most, almost all, of these kids do drugs. They feel better, are happier, when on drugs. They hang out a lot at malls and stay there for hours on end. They do not have jobs of any kind and many steal money from parents and siblings. Most of these kids are not aggressive individually. In a group setting they are usually not aggressive but are louder and follow easily. They are susceptible to being recruited by drug dealers, who cruise malls looking for just these types of kids.

These kids are our future high school dropouts. And for a few, our future drug dealers and hookers.

What to do? Get Parents/Guardians involved - BUT! I talked with one single parent and she advised not to get Children and Family Services involved because it would look bad on her and she has 2 other younger kids to look after as well. So the oldest (15) troubled boy is left to fend for himself. And he left home and is one of the invisible kids who stays with friends here and there and misses classes and exams at school.

Great...so some parents don't want to get involved helping their kids when everything they have tried doesn't work. Most parents are too close to be objective, and fall back to yelling and berating the kid. That is why an outside person can be of great help. The person can listen objectively to both parents and teen and recommend a course of action. Children and Family

Services people have the expertise, if only they were called. School councilors are another great resource who, for the most part, are ignored by parents even if the teen has asked them for help.

This problem cannot be fixed overnight, but I believe it can be fixed.
As usual though, parents really need to help too. The resources are there, the kids want help - who is holding the bag?

Well, we could start by building the self esteem of these kids. We could start by providing a safe place where these kids could gather and just be themselves. We could provide a kid hostel for kids who don't want to live at home, and don't want to live on the street. We could create a Facebook friends page in their support. We could create local YouTube videos on coping strategies and other topics relevant and appropriate to these kids. We could...

Time is slipping by and the kids are still out there. Perhaps we could start with just one kid. Then that teen tells another, and perhaps word of mouth will help create a new fostering, helpful environment for these kids. But, they still need a place to go to, other than a mall.

Is there a solution? Of course, but it is not a single solution. It is a multi-part approach. One student - many resources.

First things first. Most of these kids have given up, and I don't say that lightly. We need to turn that around, and we can, if we care enough. Will the teen listen? With the right, or appropriate approach, I believe the answer is yes. That means being open-minded, and start with open-ended statements and questions. A smile and a soft voice go a long way too.

This topic can go on and on but let's start here and add to it as we go along.

Good listening...

CH 5 : SUICIDE

Suicide by Death - Suicide Contagion

Most young people who commit suicide want a release. Quite often the eulogy for the dead student will wax sentimentality with flowery, loving and misunderstanding words.
Sometimes other students listening to the kind words which no one has ever said about them, wish they could be thought of the same way; instead of the harmful way they perceive it to be presently.
Sometimes a hypnosis-like change takes place in a student who was a good friend of the dead student, a confidant of a tearful friend, or was at a school assembly notification, or was at the funeral of a student who died by suicide.

Sometimes that student will go home and kill themselves. Sometimes the same way as the suicide victim did. It can happen as soon as getting home without even speaking with anyone. Suicide by death - of another.

There is a name for it now. It is recognized. It is something for mental health professionals to be aware of when a student dies by their own hand.

The name is Suicide Contagion.

http://www.cmaj.ca/content/early/2013/05/21/cmaj.1213
77

An article from the CBC references the study.

http://www.cbc.ca/news/health/story/2013/05/21/suicide
-contagion-school.html

Don't let the numbers and words never heard before throw you off. The study appears to be for peers. On the other hand, the CBC article breaks it down very well.

The gist is - a theory of more student suicides and attempted suicides after a student commits suicide is less a theory now and more of a not well understood, but accepted, condition. Enough to raise alarms and suggest different approaches for student mental health support following a death incident. The younger the kids, the more vulnerable.
We must see all of you students now, ask the questions, reassure that confidential help is ready and most important, that trust is assured. Permissions from the student should be gained before the session starts.

I didn't see anything mentioned about student depression vulnerability regarding an accidental death of a student. However I suspect there is a connection there as well.

We don't want you to die, our students, our kids.

We want you to live and overcome depression and enjoy more happiness again. There are new ways to help. But we need to know you want/need help before the final decision or fatal feeling is made or felt.

To your health...

Added June 30, 2013

More news stories, including one which includes a view which I had stated above. From the CBC we have this update.

Needed: New approaches to defuse 'suicide contagion' among teens

http://www.cbc.ca/news/canada/story/2013/05/22/f-suicide-contagion-prevention.html

From the article:

"There were a few things that we found really shocking — like just how many Canadian adolescents are reporting that somebody in their school has died of suicide," says Ian Colman.

The story above was linked from this story.

Youth key to helping families fight stigma of mental illness, suicide

http://www.cbc.ca/news/health/story/2013/06/28/f-youth-mental-health-awareness-suicide.html

From this article:

Getting people to talk about suicide and mental illness is not always easy. People may not wish to talk about feelings of depression. Deaths by suicide are not always publicly identified as such by families, or identified in the same way that deaths from cancer or heart disease might be described.

CH 5 : SUICIDE: THE LEGACY

The Legacy for a Dead Teen

The legacy for Jamie Hubley, a gay teen who killed himself in 2011 for a number of reasons including bullying at his high school, is getting closer to reality.

The federal government is giving 250,000 dollars to the Canadian Red Cross to have 2400 kids trained to deliver anti-bullying workshops.
Here is the story:
http://www.cbc.ca/news/health/story/2013/06/02/feds-ottawa-bullying-hubley.html

This link is similar but more into the politics:
http://www.cbc.ca/news/politics/story/2013/06/02/feds-ottawa-bullying-hubley.html

Jamie Hubley's father, Allan, put it all into perspective in a very personal way.
Act now.
Here is the family's story which appeared on CBC news last October:
Jamie Hubley's family continues fight against suicide

http://www.cbc.ca/news/canada/ottawa/story/2012/10/15/ottawa-jamie-hubley-suicide-allan-hubley.html

Valuable excerpts:
"With all due respect, I think we have enough studies, I think we have a definition on bullying ... our governments have a lot of information available to them

on bullying," Hubley said. "I don't think we need more information. ... We can't wait a year for action. What we need is action now. If there's money available we should find a way to get that into the frontline troops,"
including the Youth Services Bureau.
"We can't rely on parents to be able to watch their children every moment of the day, we can't rely on teachers to be the only ones policing the hallways of the schools and the washrooms, and you can't always have your best friend beside you," he said.
"You have a kid in crisis, you don't want to wait six hours. You want help now."
"Do something yourself to stop bullying. Don't wait for someone else to step up and do it...."

He is trying so hard to change attitudes because his son is dead. He would just like to have his son back again. Perhaps, with his impetus, another son or daughter will be saved. We all very much hope so.

Please be nice to each other - we all need it...

CH 5 : SUICIDE: BULLYING
(Added for this book edition)

Suicide – both daughters

This, like all child suicides, should not have happened. A parent's worst nightmare – times two. What are we still doing wrong?

http://www.irishcentral.com/news/Donegal-mother-to-sue-educational-authority-after-her-two-girls-took-their-own-lives-234218811.html?utm_source=outbrain&utm_medium=content&utm_campaign=paid

I personally not even imagine the pain – of the two teens – and of the parents.

CH 5 : IMPULSE SUICIDE

More on Impulse Suicide Attempts

More information on impulse, or sudden, suicide attempts for students, parents, teachers, friends and clinicians.

One of my previous posts called, "Accidental Salvation - Suicide Postponed", http://www.privsec.com/blogs/blog5.php/2012/08/06/accidental-salvation-suicide-postponed

mentioned *sudden, deep, death-thought depression*, which could have led to suicide.

Now researchers have come to some conclusions about impulse (what I called sudden) suicide attempts, and how many were successful compared to premeditated suicide.

From the Suicide Prevention Resource Center comes this news update: Research: Impulsivity and Suicide

http://www.sprc.org/news-events/the-weekly-spark/weekly-spark-thursday-february-7-2013?utm_source=Weekly+Spark+February+7%2C+2012&utm_campaign=Weekly+Spark+February+7+2013&utm_medium=email

The announcement reads:
Researchers from the University of Pennsylvania and LaSalle University warn that focusing on depression and

hopelessness as indicators of suicide risk may result in overlooking persons at high risk for making impulsive suicide attempts, which, according to their research, are as likely to result in death as premeditated attempts. Compared to persons making premeditated suicide attempts, persons making impulsive attempts have lower expectations that their attempt will be fatal, less depression and hopelessness, less of a likelihood of a history of childhood sexual abuse, and a higher likelihood of an alcohol use disorder. The authors warn clinicians not to "assume that a person is not at risk for making an impulsive attempt if he or she does not exhibit impulsivity as a general personality trait," since research indicates that people making impulsive suicide attempts do not necessarily score high on impulsivity tests.

The authors also found that "There were no statistically significant differences between individuals who made an impulsive attempt and those who made a premeditated attempt on any demographic characteristics (i.e. gender, race, marital status, employment status, education level)." This research used data from subjects who were "recent suicide attempters participating in a preliminary or full clinical trial investigating the use of cognitive therapy in reducing repeat suicide attempts." Of these subjects, 43 percent had made an impulsive attempt (that is, reporting no premeditation prior to the attempt) and 36 percent had made a premeditated attempt (that is, had contemplated for three hours or more prior to making an attempt). The remaining 21 percent "reported considering suicide for three hours or less prior to the attempt" and were excluded from the data analysis.

Spokas, M., Wenzel, A., Brown, G. K., & Beck, A. T. (2012). Characteristics of individuals who make impulsive suicide attempts. Journal of Affective Disorders, 136(3), 1121-1125.

Understanding aspects of the human condition is always ongoing. Learning takes place. And, most of the time, we are better for it. This is very encouraging research. Students need to see this.

Hopefully, students will be helped before personal disaster takes place. But, somebody - someone - had to understand, and help. The student needs to accept help. Together, student and helper, the mind and heart can be helped to heal. There is a future again.

Live for another day, day after day...

CH 5 : SUICIDE:BULLYING: VIGILANTE

Anti-Social Vigilante backlash killing and ruining young lives

Anti-Social vigilante backlash is killing and ruining young lives. Do we hear about the ruined lives after being exploited on the internet? After the truth comes out? No. In almost all cases, there are no apologies. In one case mentioned below a boy died after being falsely accused by attackers using internet "social" media.

Social networking is really anti-social networking when used for the wrong purposes.

The vigilante mindset, which includes the "*I want to be first to accuse or out someone*" syndrome, is rampant. And, apparently the perpetrators don't learn from one incident to the next.

I say it again. Some kids die because of it. Others have their lives ruined. Usually nobody talks about them or their families - the innocents, the falsely accused.

The internet has given rise to instant power for people who shouldn't have it at all. They are not mature enough to use it wisely.

Let's look at some very high profile cases of teen sex, bullying and suicide. And most of all, who to blame.

Amanda Todd in British Columbia killed herself. My

blogs about this sad event which should not have happened are here

http://www.privsec.com/blogs/blog5.php/2012/10/13/dead-too-little-too-late

here

http://www.privsec.com/blogs/blog5.php/2012/10/16/student-death-and-the-frenzy-syndrome

and here

http://www.privsec.com/blogs/blog5.php/2012/10/17/students-so-many-bullied-so-many-hurt

The vigilantes named a young person

http://www.vancouversun.com/technology/Mother+Amanda+Todd+accused+tormentor+lashes+online+lynch/7400380/story.html

as the person who had the influence over her, that is, was blackmailing her. He was innocent. But he received death threats and nasty internet attention. The police were methodically investigating the case so as to charge the right person if charges were deemed appropriate and if charges were seen to have a chance of successful prosecution in court. But the police were not fast enough for the internet trolls who just wanted to cause hurt to whomever "they" thought "had to be" guilty.
Of course the bullying is perpetuated by other students or trolls to begin with.

The next case is that of Rehtaeh Parsons

http://www.privsec.com/blogs/blog5.php/2013/04/14/the
-death-of-rehtaeh-parsons

Blaming the kids (one-sided story) and going public. Ok,
now the vigilantes step in, with a passion. The boys are
identified. Four boys, according to the mother.
And finally, the truth comes out, although a mess. It was
consensual - not rape. And it wasn't four boys. One of
the four "identified" boys apparently wasn't even there
that night. The boys, without benefit of a trial, now have
to defend themselves from the very people who would
go after anyone without knowing anything about the
case. The accusers want their little bit of fame and
whether or not the accused are innocent doesn't seem to
matter to these people at all. The world is much more
cruel now than ever before. We need the truth, not
supposition.
The parents and family members apparently didn't want
to know that their daughter/grand-daughter was a normal
teenager with hormones and perhaps not the angel they
perceived her to be. When the "other side" of the story
started appearing, they refused to believe it. They tore
down the "two sides to every story" posters that were put
up. I wonder though, was guilt about not saving her
daughter in the bathroom the real push for revenge?
Because, in my opinion, this was a revenge act. In no
way, shape or form am I making light of a child's death.
That is one of the worst things that can ever happen. No,
I just believe revenge is not justice. Most of all, the
politicians were sucked in. The premier of Nova Scotia
made comments and suggested legislation, based on one
side of the story. Even Prime Minister Harper was

caught up.
http://www.cbc.ca/news/technology/story/2013/04/16/f-policing-social-media.html

Politicians should know better. Perhaps caught up in the "hate, blame someone frenzies"?

In California, a story around Audrie Pott who committed suicide.

http://www.foxnews.com/us/2013/04/15/family-assaulted-calif-teen-who-committed-suicide-planning-legal-action-against/?test=latestnews

This case actually looks legitimate. But the other side of the story "MUST" be heard!

Marjorie Raymond in Quebec
Bullying - Student and Adult - Sorrow and Death in the News

http://www.privsec.com/blogs/blog5.php/2011/12/05/bullying-student-and-adult-sorrow-death

Jamie Hubley in Ontario
Bullying in Ontario - Apples and Oranges

http://www.privsec.com/blogs/blog5.php/2011/12/02/bullying-in-ontario-apples-and-oranges

After the Boston bombing (where 20,000 runners, family and supporters were trying to use cell phones at the same time and over-powered the cellular network system) the arm-chair know-it-alls started accusing people of being the bomber. It did not take long for the police to surmise it was more than one person. The police investigation was fast, accurate and thorough. They wanted to get the right perpetrators. However the Reddit vigilantes named someone they thought was the culprit. This particular boy, Sunil Tripathi, was found dead in a river after leaving his effects and a note behind. He had disappeared the same day he was named. I suppose the folks using Reddit are happy they are responsible for the death of an innocent person. They seemed happy to name him.

One-way thinking. How many more deaths will there be and how many more innocent kids accused, because of these internet-ready social media abusers. They are the biggest bullies of all.

http://www.cbc.ca/news/yourcommunity/2013/04/reddit-apologizes-for-boston-bombing-witch-hunt.html

http://www.foxnews.com/us/2013/04/24/authorities-say-body-found-in-river-could-be-missing-brown-student/

http://www.foxnews.com/us/2013/04/25/officials-body-found-in-water-off-providence-park-that-missing-brown-student/?test=latestnews

Nice going. Basically, in my opinion, the Reddit and Twitter users killed this boy.

Why did this happen? Don't let it happen again!

What to do if cyber-bullying finds you as a victim

http://www.cbc.ca/news/canada/manitoba/story/2013/04/22/mb-needhelpnow-anti-cyberbullying-website.html

It is an article about a new support website for sexting issues and, well, see for yourself here.
http://needhelpnow.ca/app/en/

Those intimate pictures were established through a trust relationship. Don't pass them around. Don't use them to show off. Teens are teens. Don't be malicious to each other.
Have fun, oh yes, and joke around, sure, but don't let it become malicious. Then it's mean, low, cowardly and bullying.

Possible Solutions!

Ban social media
background check before allowed to use social media
Class smart phones as weapons
Don't give weapons to 5 year olds, or teens or adults who act like 5 year olds
Create amazing legislation - not really - dull, workable legislation already exists - we need an educational response/solution/thought/action/consideration/consultation

Actually promote healthy relationships at school
Google, Facebook, Tumblr, Reddit, et al should promote
good citizenship on the net
Add you own suggestions

Part of the problem is kids not "fitting in". Yet they want
to. Kids - Trying to Fit In

http://www.privsec.com/blogs/blog5.php/2012/10/30/kid
s-trying-to-fit-in

I, and many others, have covered how kids can get
"well" again by getting their confidence back and feeling
better about themselves.
Student Mind Restart for Depression Sickness

http://www.privsec.com/blogs/blog5.php/2012/11/12/stu
dent-mind-restart-for-depression-sick

I've talked about kids who believe the only way out or
solution is to kill themselves.
Kids - Self Termination

http://www.privsec.com/blogs/blog5.php/2012/08/29/kid
s-self-termination

Sometimes kids feel they are not wanted anymore.
Kids or Adults: Broken and not wanted anymore

http://www.privsec.com/blogs/blog5.php/2012/05/05/bro
ken-and-not-wanted-anymore

Sometimes people bully to get revenge.
Child Bullying for Revenge

http://www.privsec.com/blogs/blog5.php/2012/03/25/child-bullying-for-revenge

It has been said that suicide is not to end life, but to end pain. This article may help you understand that others have gone before you and felt the black despair as well.
Teen Suicide - Not Sharing the Pain

http://www.privsec.com/blogs/blog5.php/2011/10/23/teen-suicide-not-sharing-the-pain

The only person who can possibly help you in your depression, is the responsible, caring, thoughtful, experienced, listening person you tell. Share the pain. It actually does help, more than you would think.

Remember: Kids Help Phone - 800-668-6868

Waiting out a sudden black depression - important! Also called Impulse.
A Teenager: Almost Gone

http://www.privsec.com/blogs/blog5.php/2012/08/01/a-teenager-almost-gone

Impulse (sudden) Suicide - please read - the feeling passes quickly.
More on Impulse Suicide Attempts

http://www.privsec.com/blogs/blog5.php/2013/02/10/more-on-impulse-suicide-attempts

Do anti-bullying laws work?

Bullying Backlash: More laws beget more bullying

http://www.privsec.com/blogs/blog5.php/2011/12/17/bullying-backlash-more-laws-beget-more

Please be considerate with and to each other. That's all it takes for a better community, school, town, city,,,life...

Try smiling, it's catchy...

CH 5 : SELF TERMINATION

Kids - Self Termination

Why do some kids willfully, consciously, studiously and calmly terminate their future?

I think that if we knew, we could help stop the tide. We know a little from interviews with kids who attempted suicide. We don't know what the trigger is for each one. One thing that usually is part and parcel is being told something. Something not pleasant at all, which sends one into a depression from which there is no escape.

An article appeared in the Calgary Herald today written by a columnist who has three kids, who knew a young boy of twelve, named Noah, who killed himself last Thursday. Why did he kill himself? Well, to state the obvious, we cannot ask him. There was no warning. Apparently, no tell-tale signs. Dead in an instant.

Please read the article and perhaps you can help someone in need. There is always some child in need of mental help. They are not crazy, but perhaps sad, confused and uncertain.

Here is the title for the article called, "Why you should know about Noah's death" which is a dead link unfortunately. This article was also published in the Edmonton Journal, word for word.

His parents, and especially his older brother by about two years, will be experiencing grief (pain and anguish) for a long time to come. Such an experience can be soul-killing. I personally feel very sorry for them.

I feel very sorry for the boy - not why or the other W's - just for him. Sometimes there is no reason that we will know - and we desperately need a reason. It is not for us. It is for the boy who died so quickly, so young.

What is very sad is that this isn't the only twelve year old boy named Noah who killed himself near the end of August this year. The other boy's name was Noah Grawemeyer

http://ronkemp.blogspot.ca/2012/08/noah-grawemeyer-12-bullying-leads-to.html

who lived in Indiana. What is incredibly sad is that this is the tip of the iceberg - only what is reported in the news.

For those left behind, the pain comes in waves, with many little things triggering the emotions. Mental help is needed. Repercussions will be long-term. This was a decision point over which they had no control or fore-knowledge. Now decision points abound, and feelings, not knowledge or logic, will prevail.

At the end of the article written by Dave Budge are two help phone numbers which can be called for help when the mental anguish becomes more than we can bare. The Kids Help Phone is one I have promoted throughout many posts here. If you need to talk, or just express your feelings, please help yourself by calling the folks at the other end of the help line numbers.

Here is the rub: most kids who are becoming suicidal don't even know about any form of help being available, no charge and anonymous.

So how do we learn from this and help those who need help, before it is too late for them?

We've said it before and we say it again, education in schools. Everyone becomes sad at one time or another. However if ALL the kids know there is help available then it is very possible that the child will call help from the stranger, when it is needed. One other issue is that most kids don't know when it is "needed". They think they can handle it. Most of the time they can "get along" handle it, but not all the time. Will they call when it - their depression, whether quick or long term, becomes so deep and unwieldy that they can no longer "control" it? Unfortunately, not always.

For you kids who are hurting - talk with someone. You would be amazed how good it feels. The person you talk to doesn't have to say anything. Just listen, that's all. When you go silent, they may gently prompt you to say more, if you wish to then. From time to time we all need someone who will just listen, because from time to time we all need to talk out depressive thoughts.

The mental state leading up to suicide is the point of decision from calm to desperation. It's like flipping a switch. You care, you don't care. About yourself, your life, your future, your friends, your family. The switch quite often is associated with the mental state of yes/no. When all is said and done, it can be that simple. One more day or no. One more hour or no. One more minute or no. Actually time isn't meaningful at this point. Only "now" is meaningful. And, only stopping the pain is meaningful.

Help us who care, help you. Here is the Kids Help Phone number.

Kids Help Phone at 1-800-668-6868

http://www.kidshelpphone.ca/teens/home/splash.aspx

You know what to do - call...

Please help - you...

CH 5 : SUICIDE: BULLYING: REHTAEH PARSONS

The Death of Rehtaeh Parsons

The death of a Nova Scotia teenager has come to the attention of the world. She had lived in a very small town and attended school at Cole Harbour District High School. Kids in small towns do party from time to time and perhaps have too much to drink or smoke. Good judgement is overpowered and things happen. In most small towns, secrets are kept and put away. In my small town District Collegiate High School many years ago, there were many instances of incest that were mentioned and never talked about again. Even if the teachers found out, it was never brought up. It was buried. There was no bullying because of it. That was then.

Now bullying, hurtful behaviour or writing or saying, is the norm. It seems that some kids want to see how much pain, hurt or agony they can inflict on another. Why? Power trip? A laugh? A "watch this"?

Bullying for any reason, whether sex, physical size, mental challenges or any other reason that one person believes they are superior over another, is not acceptable - at all. I believe that what happened to Rehtaeh Parsons, after getting together with friends that one night, was bullying although not thought of as that at the time, which then became a bullying "game", without thought of consequence - for anyone. The fact that she was an "A" student perhaps caused some jealousy as well, and when an opportunity came up to hurt her, well it was used by those who were learning-challenged.

This wasn't just one or two people saying things or texting her. Over time, it was many.

I still strongly believe in education, right from wrong, in a way students understand and can embrace.
You can't beat people over the head with your message. Saying, "Thou shalt not Bully", would only work for a very few. Instead, appeal to the heart, then mind. Show (describe in adjective-laden detail) the mental collapse from beginning to end. Show the outward signs which depression can cause. Walk among your audience. Make eye contact. Make your presentation so powerful, yet humble, that they really want to listen. Listening begets understanding. Be a storyteller, not a statistical replay nerd.

The original story was published in the Chronicle Herald in Halifax, by Selena Ross. It is a powerful story which appears to be written from the heart.
Here are some excerpts:
Rehtaeh spent the past year and a half trying to handle the fallout from that night, said her mother...
For one thing, social media can be toxic, said the mother. After Rehtaeh left her school, other kids were relentless.
"People texted her all the time, saying 'Will you have sex with me?'" she remembered. "Girls texting, saying 'You're such a slut.'"
On March 3, Rehtaeh posted a photo of herself on Facebook next to a quote from Martin Luther King Jr.:
"In the end, we will remember not the words of our enemies, but the silence of our friends."

I know that for most folks reading my blog, I am "preaching to the converted" as they say. If we could just get the kids to think as another for a few seconds, maybe there would be more understanding.

If you don't have any problems, it's hard to imagine how it feels to have problems, whether physical or emotional.

If the kids had known then what they know now, would they have done the wrong? I don't think so. Perhaps that is the question kids should ask themselves before picking on another student - what is the "could be" consequence?

There have been a lot of suicides among students (who just wanted the persecution and pain to go away) because of thoughtless actions by others. Most kids who make mistakes (all kids?) just want to be forgiven and accepted. Is that so hard to do for another?

I sincerely hope the kids learn, and perhaps become ambassadors for common sense.

Added April 27, 2013
Until you know all sides of the story, it is never what you thought it was.

Edited for this student book edition.

CH 5 : HIDDEN IN THE NIGHT

Hidden in the Night

This may be the last post about bullying and suicide for a while. It is too painful to see it, and more, understand it. "Understand it" is a big statement - yes, I do understand.

The "night" for many people is all the time. I think by the time you get to the end of this post you will see the hidden.

This is a brutal look at the result of school violence, home violence, emotionally berated, and any other way to make a person feel bad and have power over them. So many people are victims, children as victims - who cannot protect themselves. They do not have the knowledge or experience to do so. But they have the experience and knowledge of violence to themselves. In some cases, they know nothing else.

Education in the home environment is not really an option, now or ever. Yes, there are ads on radio and TV and the occasional billboards. There are many informational websites, but they will not be visited by these uncaring and vicious parents and "care" givers.

In school, there are more programs for kids. There is school and local, state/provincial/federal anti-bullying legislation. Most of these "laws" DO NOT WORK. Intelligent school presentations/lectures by educators who specialize in cause and consequence of bullying are effective. For a while. Reinforcement of the message is desperately needed, but not recognized as needed.

A chance of hope exists. Students are "starting" to recognize the possible dire result of bullying. There are always bullies who just don't care - now or ever. But the kids who just weren't thinking before, are thinking now - of others, and how they feel.

I am going to show you the result of PAIN - STOPPING THE PAIN!

The ONE single thread through all of the kids who commit suicide is ending the pain.

If you don't want to feel, don't want to cry, don't want to act - read this post no further.

From YouTube, where so many have created tributes to those close to them, who have killed themselves because they wanted the pain to STOP.

* Suicide Note written by my little sister, Raven.
* A Real Attempted Suicide Note
* My little girls suicide note.
* She was Bullied to death R.I.P

This all goes back to my premise that to make the pain go away, forever, you kill yourself.

Intervention is possible - if - someone who is trusted is told. The healing process cannot normally be done alone. Survive alone, yes. Heal alone, no.

Again, we must be more conscious of others actions and tell-tale signs of emotional problems. It is very hard to do. The signs are usually quite well hidden.. But try, we must.

Back to education. Not the "normal" school education but more the education of mind and body as part of a group of peers, who actually care about each other.

I hope we can turn the tide someday.

Good learning...Good feeling...

CH 5 : TEEN SUICIDE –
NOT SHARING THE PAIN

Teen Suicide - Not Sharing the Pain

It has been said that suicide is not to end life, but to end pain.

In a previous article about personality disorders I made reference to goldbrickers, fakers. What I write about today is not fake and the many teens experiencing deep emotional pain are in real trouble.

In a previous article Student Self-destruct, I touched on self-harm and help resources.

http://www.privsec.com/blogs/blog5.php/2011/06/12/student-self-destruct

For students today, there is much more opportunity for emotional pain than ever before. Teens can be picked on through the internet, social networking sites, email.

The recent suicide of a young Ottawa boy brings it home. What really brings it home is his blog, which at the moment of this writing, is still up. Here is a newspaper article, which in turn references other papers and articles and the blog itself.

http://www.huffingtonpost.com/2011/10/17/jamie-hubley-commits-suicide_n_1015646.html.
The blog, at http://catchmeblondy.tumblr.com/ (taken down a week after), has mature subject matter and

language. Why do we say that when it is a 15 year old who wrote it and the blog is read by other teens. I really don't know. Perhaps, more for the parents.

11/11/19: His blog is gone, here is a tribute blog

http://www.tumblr.com/tagged/catchmeblondy

and another one here.

http://www.tumblr.com/tagged/catchmeblondy?before=1 318896357

This is his last blog entry

http://www.privsec.com/blogs/media/blogs/edu/Last_Po st-You_cant_break_When_youre_already_broken.txt

a few days before he died.

A Facebook page was set up in honor of the boy, Jamie. Too late though. So many didn't know.

Bullying seems to have played a role, but to what extent, no one is sure now. Self-harm was admitted to as well - cutting.

Death is forever. That may sound obvious, but for many teens it is not. It is a long dreamless sleep that you don't have to wake from.

Teens have killed themselves for generations. In the past, it was never attributed. Now it is.

If the pain had been shared with a caring person, or even a total stranger, it may end differently. Sometimes the total stranger can help in ways not possible with a friend, peer, parent or counselor.

But sharing the pain has to begin with the person feeling it. Many teens want people to mind-read them, and are so disappointed when it doesn't happen. Reaching out by blog, phone call, email or just getting a chance to talk face-to-face with another person is so important. However, social sites are not a good idea.

A fairly radical change of behaviour or lifestyle is usually indicative of mental or emotional issues that cannot be dealt with by the teen. Physical indicators are gaining or losing noticeable weight over a short period of time. Mood swings and self-harm can be observed as well.

To those who see the changes and realize there is a problem, we can offer help, usually by committing to active listening participation, which can be most important.

I once had a friend that I knew in childhood and as an adult and he had attempted suicide five or six times by the time he was sixteen. The last time, at sixteen, landed him in the hospital in a coma for a week. Those were the days when it was not talked about, ever. There was no internet, email, etc. There was the telephone and getting together in person only. Why was he so depressed? He would not share that for many years. But share one day he did. He had been assaulted when he was six years old and the assaults continued while he was seven. The family moved to a different province and city and it stopped. He was given a dog which he fell in love with. They were inseparable. About a year later the dog was run over in their quiet neighbourhood. He was picked up from school that day by both parents. He should have known there was something wrong. He was told on the way home. The body of the dog was in the garage. He ran to the dog and hugged the crushed lifeless body and cried and cried. He went in the house. The depression that his dog had helped so much to dispel came back with a vengeance and lasted for the next 8 years. He was never "right" after that. He never cried again. He forgot his childhood, as if it had never existed. He was mostly an automation. He did manage to control his thoughts and emotions but not until he was in his twenties. It still took decades to really get a grip on living. This is a person who never had help and yet managed to survive. He said though that survival has not ever been a top priority, but that he would not consciously try to kill himself after the last time at sixteen.

Is teen depression a problem? Oh yes. Not the blip in an otherwise good emotional state. We are talking a severe, as in long-lasting, depression. The longer it lasts, the more one thinks that there is no out. If the good days outnumber the bad days, there seems to be a hole, or a way out. However, if the bad days continue, with rejection, bullying, deterrence, discouragement, dismay, intimidation, scaring - well, the depression can become so deep and all-encompassing that the teen is like a zombie - existing without feeling. Unfortunately, when feeling returns, it returns with a huge impact and force, and that can indeed be the last straw. It then becomes just easier to end the pain, for good.

What does fatal depression feel like? It doesn't. There is an absence of feeling. There is only a decision made and relief that it is done. Actually a sense of peace, an evening out, no destiny, no future, no people, no things, no day, no night - just slipping away into nothing. Not even blackness, just, nothing. I don't know how else to describe it. I suppose one has to be there and survive to know what nothing is.

Teens are really good at hiding their depression from others. But once alone, it all comes out.

Showing and sharing yourself, who you are, is incredibly scary and requires courage. Telling your story (feelings) to another requires courage, or desperation. But sometimes, in desperation, the wrong choice is made. Jamie's pain was exacerbated by the shunning and rejection due to coming out of the closet and openly admitting he was gay. The only one in school. This day in age it is still not a good idea to admit openly that you are gay. If you like being hit, spit at, cursed, threatened, ostracized, looked down upon, laughed at, made fun of and so on then sure. But in most parts of the country, no, not a good idea.

Can bullying be legislated away? Nope. There are probably more bullies now than ever before. They have simply gone "underground". Laws were made for adults, which kids are also supposed to follow. Hmmm, perhaps we need kid laws. Here is an interesting snippet from Edmonton Public School Board regarding student behaviour.

http://www.epsb.ca/policy/ig.bp.shtml

3. Students shall show respect for:
school authority;
others and their property;
ethnic, racial, religious, and gender differences;
school attendance and punctuality;
work habits, assignments and homework;
school property;
textbooks and equipment;
fire alarms and safety equipment; and
district policies relating to smoking, alcohol, drugs and inhalants.
Most students don't care. In schools today, there is sensitivity training. Really.

Some pundits say, "It gets better". No, it doesn't.

The only person who can possibly help you in your depression, is the person you tell. Share the pain. It actually does help, more than you would think.

Remember: Kids Help Line - 800-668-6868

Good listening... Good understanding...

By the way, here is the Edmonton Public School Board official suicide policy called, "Edmonton Public Schools Board Policies and Regulations - Student or Staff Suicide".

http://www.epsb.ca/policy/ihcf.ar.shtml

It seems more of a butt-covering document than anything else.

Please see this interesting article as well, Pediatrician urges no blame for bullying

http://www.cbc.ca/news/health/story/2011/10/06/ns-bullying-no-blame.html

And this article, should bullying be considered a hate crime?

http://www.cbc.ca/thecurrent/episode/2011/09/29/bullying-hate-crime/

In my opinion - no. It's a superiority attitude with no patience for perceived inferior beings. Basically, a learned attitude.

Some say bullying is a "public health problem". What have they been smoking? Get a grip.

Dr. Mike

CH 6 : STUDENT MENTAL HEALTH

<u>Student Mental Health - CISD</u>

The phrase "good mental health" could be an oxymoron. Well, when people say/image/hear *mental health*, it is usually because a person has a mental health problem. We don't say to someone, "wow, you have really good mental health!". However we certainly use the term "mental health" in the context of bad, poor, at risk, depressed, disorder, etc.

Many provincial and state K-12 education jurisdictions have an interest and policy regarding student mental health.

Here is an excerpt from a page at the Alberta Ministry of Education called, <u>Mental Health in Schools</u>. The link is broken ☹ It seemed to include all vectors and most possible interchange possibilities for a student. I don't believe it is possible. But it is an incredible gesture on behalf of government. Students have the opportunity. Will they all take it? By the government's own statistics, the answer is no.

"Mental health affects many aspects of our lives. It influences how we think and feel about ourselves and others. It also affects our ability to cope with change and adapt to major life events. On any given day, 20% of students in a classroom will suffer from a mental health problem serious enough to warrant support and services. Of those, 70% will NOT receive any supports or services. These mental health issues can shape and

impact academic outcomes, behaviours, as well as the school environment "

Although Big Brother is watching, there are not enough resources to intervene in all cases. For many students, there is no escape from a "troubled" (mental abuse, physical abuse, sexual abuse, unwanted, ignored, etc.) childhood already experienced and denied.

Mental health problems will always be with us - student or adult.

We need to be aware that there are those who need help and may actually want help. Are we ready to help? Are resources available to provide ongoing support instead of a disinterested one-of interview?

Well, a lot of emphasis is applied to Concept. What about the person needing help? Unless there is a threat of some kind, the person falls through the cracks and is quite often ignored as not having a "real" mental health problem. Really, and who decided that? A "mental health professional"? Most likely not. However the problem is that the student with a mental "problem" is very vulnerable to any type of negative feedback and very likely will not try to get help again, for fear of rejection or being slighted.

Really, what we need to do is train ALL of us as **mental health first responders**...
A one or two day modified Critical Incident Stress Debriefing (CISD) course would probably do the trick. Could it be added to the school curriculum? Yes. *But*

will it be added?
Peer aged kids are usually the first to know of a mental health problem that another student is experiencing. It is my belief that the modified CISD course will give each student "mental health first responder" knowledge of action/reaction/listening/learning/response/support.

Perhaps less talk and more action is now in order. It has been studied, processed, conferenced, webcasted, facilitated, moderated, blogged and talked to death. Action please.

Good CIS learning...

CH 6 : KIDS COPING AFTER A DISASTER

Kids Coping after a Disaster

Most kids have excellent coping skills. It usually doesn't take long before they are back to playing again and being able to laugh again after a disaster.

For the kids who don't adapt well, here are some Critical Incident Stress signs to watch for to help parents help their kids, which are published on the website of the Search and Rescue Society of British Columbia. The no-nonsense articles concern children
http://www.sarbc.org/sarbc/ciskid1.html

and adolescents
http://www.sarbc.org/sarbc/ciskid2.html

Both articles were written by Raymond Lafond. Please see the end of each article for proper attribution.

Here are some excerpts from the article for parents of children:
Bedtime problems are the most frequently reported difficulties encountered by parents following a disaster. Children may refuse to go to bed alone and may insist on sleeping with their parents, or having someone present in their room. They may suddenly be terrified of the dark or of animals. Once asleep, they may have terrible nightmares during which they relive the disaster, then wake up crying and screaming.
If your child wakes up frightened, go and comfort him or

her immediately. When you go in, try not to turn on bright lights or talk in a loud voice. Acknowledge the fear: "Your must have had a very scary dream." Listen without interruption to what your child has to say about his or her dream. Do not deny the existence of fear by saying, "There's nothing to be afraid of"; rather, be accepting, understanding, and help the child express the fear and gain greater control over it. To calm your child it is essential to help establish what is real and what is fantasy. By allowing the child to describe the nightmare, you will have an opportunity to determine which fears are real or imaginary. When the child has told you about the nightmare, acknowledge and validate the experience by saying: "It must have seemed real to you," or " that sounds like a very scary experience, I don't blame you for hiding ... crying ... screaming ... running away ... " Reassure the child that you are near and that he or she is safe. If possible, stay until your child falls asleep.

For parents of adolescents, here are some excerpts: *Threats or attempts to injure or kill oneself are not uncommon among adolescents, and any indication of suicidal feelings must be taken seriously. The most frequent motivation is loss of close family or friends. Feelings of helplessness, hopelessness, and worthlessness are strong indicators of potential suicide, expressed verbally or non-verbally through behavioural signs (withdrawal, antisocial behaviour, loss of interest, apathy and agitation), physical symptoms (sleep and appetite disturbances), and cognitive process changes (perceived loss of alternatives, poor judgement and reasoning ability). Evidence of caring and concern are*

the most immediate and effective ways workers can help. In general, however, any person with suicidal thoughts should be referred for professional help.
A trouble sign that requires immediate attention is confusion (regressive behaviour, inappropriate feeling, immobilization), and generally implies a deep-seated disturbance that should probably be referred to a mental health professional.

Kids can cope better than parents or adults. Kids can be incredibly adaptable. Again, more so that many adults.

This is for kids - it's ok - you will feel. You will go through many different feelings, including possibly anger, and you may outburst to others who are also experiencing their own mixed-up feelings. Try to go easy on each other. You don't have to cover it up. You are tough - you survived. Let go with someone you trust. Trust! Please read my missive to parents. It covers debriefing, for you. Your peers may be the first ones you talk it over with. The professional can try to help you out of the quagmire you may find yourself in.

For parents, when you finally pay attention to the kids, look for signs of distress in your children. It may very well be not obvious at first. Keep the kids in mind when you are trying to cope - it's not just about you, parents. Your kid's negative memories will last longer and have more impact than you think. Professional, especially experienced, Critical Incident Stress debriefers are really valuable after a disaster. Try to make sure your kids get a chance to have a session (talk, conversation, debrief) with this experienced person. By experienced, I mean one who had gone through their own disaster feeling and response, as well as appropriate training to help others who have experienced similar loss, and recognize that no two people will ever experience the same disaster the same way, with the same feelings and expression of their feelings.

Good learning...

CH 6 : STUDENT SELF-DESTRUCT

<u>Student Self-Destruct</u>

Sometimes during a student's life, a depression will occur which will seem to be never-ending, over-powering and mentally paralyzing. Sometimes a student will deliberately hurt themselves just to feel, or as a way to ask for help.

Here is an article which may help because you will understand that you are not alone, and that help is available for you, if you just reach out. From the CBC, comes this report called, "<u>Self-harm hospitalizes 17,000 a year</u>".

<u>http://www.cbc.ca/thecurrent/episode/2011/09/29/bullying-hate-crime/</u>

A quote from the article:
More than 45 Canadians are hospitalized every day due to self-injury and many of those are 15 to 19 years old...

Where to go for help? Hard to find out isn't it?

Try this site (they also have a toll-free phone number - 800-668-6868), <u>Kids Help Phone</u>.

<u>http://www.kidshelpphone.ca/Teens/AskUsOnline.aspx</u>

See my <u>previous blog post</u> for more information.

<u>http://www.privsec.com/blogs/blog5.php/2011/05/27/are-you-ready-for-kids-help-phone</u>

Reach out - Try it - You may save your sanity - or your life

CH 6 : STUDENT MIND RESTART

<u>Student Mind Restart for Depression Sickness</u>

Student Mind Restart for Depression Sickness (aka Getting it Back)

Self-worth, self-esteem (confidence), self-confidence, self-belief, self.
Yes, these all have to do with you, self.
There comes a time, which can happen more than once, when your "self" experiences a mental sickness. The sickness can be started by another or by you (yourself) thinking self-defeating thoughts leading to a chronic depression.

"Self" is everywhere - it is a powerful word. It usually means all of you, or sometimes just the inner you. When we say I'm being sorry for myself - we really mean my "self"

Here are more words with "self" as part of the word or phrase:
self-organized
self-assessment
self-control
self-upgrade
self-publishing
self-harming
self-serve
self-portrait

self-help
self-motivation
self-improvement
self-empowerment
self-discipline
self-health
self-pity
self-defense
self-management
self-doubt
self-sabotage
self-destructive
self-cutting
self-medication
self-balance
self-respect
self-growth
self-employed
self-exam
self-care
self-guide
self-development
self-imposed
self-interest
self-repair
self-storage
self-reported
self-image
self-taught
self-confidence
self-relief
self-growth

Words associated with "self":
resolution
personal strength
despondent
willpower
vitality
persistence
distrust
patience
pretty self
handsome self
healthy self
old self
changed self
inner self
know yourself

Taking back your life - Getting it back

In programming, setting _init() to start with a new or changed $self, the old associations are destroyed. Items are added individually. Hmmm. Maybe a lesson here?

How to get it back? Here is an answer. It is not a ten page article. It is one paragraph. It may seem simple - it is. Simplicity usually works.

Get involved in something creative. It becomes yours - your touch, your mind shaping your expression. It belongs to you. It is yours. It is you. And, you will finally really like you - your self.

If people try to put you down instead of saying, WOW -

they are jealous that they cannot do it. Or perhaps they are just too lazy to try it. Either way, you ARE doing it and it is all yours.

Here are stories of people who have successfully taken their lives back. From bullying and depression to feeling good about themselves, what they do and who they do it for. They made the difference, with help, re-establishing their self-esteem and self-confidence - getting it back.

Straight from my art: Bullied as teens, four young people found artistic outlets for their feeling – Edmonton Journal – dead link – search for the title for more info

Arts good outlet for feelings, experts say feeling – Edmonton Journal – dead link – search for the title for more info

'Despair would be a good word to describe it,' says bullied teen feeling – Edmonton Journal – dead link – search for the title for more info

Songwriting offered teen chance to learn about himself feeling – Edmonton Journal – dead link – search for the title for more info

Lyrics deal with good, bad, ugly - Edmonton Journal – dead link – search for the title for more info

And let's not forget Johnathan and Charlotte on Britain's Got Talent.
http://en.wikipedia.org/wiki/Jonathan_and_Charlotte

And finally, two sites which deal with you fading from

sight and thought - almost invisible.
http://www.livyjeanne.com/Invisible.html

http://waitingontimeagain.tumblr.com/post/2491672287
8/almost-invisible

I found this quick guide for you. It may resonate with
you and help you, or not. Worth looking at though.
Self-Confidence Lost? 5 Steps to Getting It Back

http://www.dawnlennon.com/2011/08/22/self-
confidence-lost-5-steps-to-getting-it-back/

Take the first step. You would be amazed how many
people are ready, willing and able to help you help your
"self".

CH 6 : TRYING TO FIT IN

<u>Kids - Trying to Fit In</u>

Yes, most kids do try to fit in, even if they say they don't. Some go to great lengths. They do it because they don't want to be left behind, ignored, forgotten.

It seems the greatest fear is to be forgotten.

Kid does want to be different and sometimes making a difference is their way to do it. Most kids need a little help from older kids or adults, to guide them gently and show them options they may not have thought of or seen yet.

Contrary to popular opinion, kids do not know everything yet. Soon :) Then, as new adults, they start learning what they didn't know that they didn't know.

Fitting in isn't about school, sex or drugs. It is about attitude. And home influences during the early years, and continuing into the pre-teen and teen years. Fitting in can start with just one other person.
Some kids who don't seem to fit in, really don't want to fit in. It may be because they don't want to play the games others are playing, or just that their mental or emotional age is so much different. Quite often fitting in means sharing a common bond or goal or experience. The kids who don't fit in and who are nevertheless memorable, will of course not be forgotten.

So, how to not be forgotten? One simple way is to be a

true friend - to someone.

Always Learning...

CH 6 : A TEENAGER: ALMOST GONE

A Teenager: Almost Gone

Once upon a time there was a troubled teenager. Well, that pretty well describes most teens at one time or another. And, that is my point. What I describe can happen to almost anyone. If it does, there is no apparent explanation. Words like, "it was so unexpected" or "he/she seemed so happy" or other words describing the perceived positive mental state of the one who is lost are said by the unknowing.

A person who is depressed now and then or actually has swings back and forth or up and down or happy and sad, may have an episode that they will not understand and will still act on. What it is, is a sudden black depression which sets you to cry and you want to just stick a knife in your arm and be done with it.
The strange thing is that the very sad feeling passes almost as quickly as it appeared. Wow, what if you had done something to yourself during that time? Well, some kids do. And that is so sad because it didn't have to be. At this time it does take someone to talk to, just for a few seconds; a caring look, a few kind words, and all is suddenly ok again. If there is no one, then bad things can happen. Death is waiting, not very patiently.

Can you recognize this sudden, black, dark depression? Can you see it coming? No, not usually. I know that is not helpful. Let me offer what is hopeful.
Now that you know this can happen, even to the most

optimistic and happy person, then you also know that you can *wait it out*. That non-action, will be the hardest thing you ever do in your life.

You will be most thankful afterward - to yourself.

My teen friend was almost gone, dead, in a blink. It wasn't what was said by another. It was what he saw in the eyes of the other, as well as the caring words. Understanding and compassion. Right then, right there. That was enough to bring him back. I hope it will be for you too.

My wish for you: happy days and no depression - again and again and again :)

CH 6 : TEEN INTERMITTENT EXPLOSIVE DISORDER

Teen Intermittent Explosive Disorder

Teen Intermittent Explosive Disorder (IED) - never heard of it? I thought not, but you will. It is the up and coming "disorder" for teens now that other "disorders" have had their fair share of publicity.

Have a look at this Edmonton Journal article called, The age of rage: psychiatrists battle over teen anger diagnosis. Link is dead unfortunately…

Mind you, this one has been around for about thirty years, but not given much attention. There are proponents who want to label most kids, and those who oppose the instant labeling of kids and who want to step back and take another look.

Towards the end of the article, there is this quote:
Dr. Allen Frances, former chair of the psychiatry department at Duke University's School of Medicine, chaired the task force that wrote the current edition of the DSM. He called IED an "unstudied" and "inherently unreliable category that probably shouldn't be in the DSM at all.
"It most certainly should not be reified into a manufactured teenage epidemic of mental disorder that is allegedly affecting millions of kids," he said.
"The suggestion that we institute prevention programs is a wildly premature over-promise until much more solid

research demonstrates that there is real need and proven effectiveness."

Also in the article there are "percentages" being bandied about. More research is required before this is categorized one way or the other.

Aren't kids labeled enough already? And, does that label follow them into adulthood?

The penchant for inventing new mental maladies, or adding new behaviours to old ones is unbelievable. Unfortunately there are those in positions of trust or power who propagate such silly things under the guise of "research" and "publishing" their thoughts, perhaps to enhance a reputation.

Well, say welcome to more mental illness. Say goodbye to common sense and peer review.

Good luck teens - you will need it in the adult world...

CH 6 : BROKEN AND
NOT WANTED ANYMORE

Kids or Adults: Broken and not wanted anymore

Sometimes you break and are not wanted anymore, by you. Sometimes something you have, or are, is violated and then is not wanted anymore. You lose interest in it, or doing it, or whatever it was at the time. Even knowing the circumstances and having knowledge of the psychology doesn't help. Why, because of the feeling - how you feel about it, or how it makes you feel. Knowing is one thing, feeling is quite another. And feeling is bad.

Welcome to the real world of emotional pain, which will take you on a course and direction hitherto not thought of or experienced until now.

The direction is unknown as is the purpose. It simply is.

This is where it gets interesting. There are no favorites anymore. Instead you have nothing to look forward to except for more pain.

You don't want that, right? Then start writing. Writing your thoughts about why the pain, what happened, when did it take place, perhaps who was involved. Eventually you will be able to say to yourself, I don't care anymore. Will the thoughts disappear? Nope. But they won't be the focus of your daily life anymore. People will notice the difference. But it is the only way to stay alive and have reasonable functionality. It is not nice or happy but it works. Eventually the edge wears off and you can function more normally, for you.

Unfortunately the hurt and pain never go away. You just forget what started or caused it. So yes, you can have pain without cause (you have actually forgotten the cause).

All hail Caesar. Tuesday is Wednesday. You are beaten down. You are like a robot. Things still get to you and bring you down even more. And you withdraw - into the only safe place left - you.

I cannot believe how messed up the world and its people are today, and this generation especially.

What is described above is going on every day for millions of people, with kids taking up the majority.

Help isn't near. There is no help. There are not enough people or shrinks in the world to help everyone. It is up to you.

How do you get out of the morass you've sunk into? Carefully. Don't scream and flail around. Deliberately focus on a safe landing and slowly and deliberately start in that direction. When you get there, which you will, examine your likes and dislikes and pick something completely new to like or get involved with. This new thing doesn't have the trappings and baggage attached to it, which only bogs you down, like some of your old things did in the past.

Does it get better? Oh yes. You don't think about it as

much. You don't sigh about it as much. The person, event or place responsible for the pain in the first place, can be re-visited again.

This post is not supposed to be cruel. It is just the way it is for most people. You have to help yourself because, most of the time, no one else will help you.

On the plus side, you can get better. Positive thoughts and feelings can, and usually do, come back. Let's just say it happens to people who thought they were immune to this degree of sadness. It can happen to anyone, at anytime. And, sometimes it is something small which sets it off.

Again though, you CAN get over it. Time is important. Something broken needs time to mend. And help. If you can find help, you are a lucky one. You will heal so much more quickly.

Good luck with this particular feeling. Nobody wants to feel broken.

Get help - this is a really, really tough one to fight off...

CH 6 : DISAPPOINTMENT AND DEPRESSION

Disappointment and Depression

Disappointment and Depression - do they go together?
Not necessarily.

However some disappointments are so big, or happen
one after the other to overwhelm us, and even the most
optimistic person can get depressed. For how long?
Well, that really depends on the person. If a person is
easily mentally crushed then depression could happen
soon and stay a while.

The key, for many people, which leads to depression is
disappointment. Girlfriend-boyfriend, parent-child,
friends, service industries, hospitals, clinics, store clerks,
government agents or clerks and the list goes on.
Disappointment could be someone being mean, or
ignoring you, or not listening, or giving don't care/bad
service or anything else which leads to *expectations not
being met*. It could be shoddy finishing work on your car
when you get it back from a shop, or it could be a
damaged item being delivered, or something else like
damage to something you value or like - which makes
you feel that people don't care about you or your car or
TV or house. The key here is feel. Your reaction, *how
you feel*, is what counts. Sometimes you can shrug it off.
Sometimes you cannot shrug it off. You internalize and a
depression is underway.

For kids, there are a lot of disappointments over time - at

144

school, playground, mall, home and with some friends. Sometimes you expect one thing and it just doesn't go right. Most disappointments don't lead to depression. But when they come fast and furious, well yes it can get very depressing. This can lead to blah - you don't want to do the activity or deal with the people that lead to the disappointment. This can lead to a number of risk activities and also leaving school.

When you are depressed, most people don't want to be around you. This could lead to further depression when alone so much.

Ok, we have some ideas why a depression can develop. Betrayed, let down, cheated, lied to, bad service/manners, can lead to feelings of disappointment - which can lead to depression.

Long term low level depression is hardly noticed by anyone else. It's just that you stop doing some things you did before, for "no apparent reason". You can be happy to the outside world and still be depressed. This can lead to "disorders" if left to itself long enough.

Now, how do we deal with it, depression and disappointment. For disappointment, talk with someone. The disappointment won't go away but it will be forgotten more easily and it will lose its value and focus. The depression will be gone as well.
For disappointment which is too big or personal to tell someone about, we need to let go. The disappointment will still be there, but we need to get past it. How to do that? Perhaps get involved in a new activity, project,

person, place - well, hopefully you realize what is being said here. When you find yourself watching the same TV shows a lot, or playing the same games a lot, or hanging around the mall a lot, then you know it's time for a change. Get happy and excited about something new to you. Perhaps it will be just what you need, or are looking for. If so, you won't even notice that the depression is gone. It will simply be gone.

We are not talking life-threatening depression here. That has been talked about before. This is the general but important, possibly life-altering, disappointment and up and down health or depression.

Occasionally, only the passage of time can help fix a *disappointment depression.*

So students and adults, know that disappoint can happen almost anytime, is usually unexpected and is thought-consuming.
If you what-if situations beforehand you may be somewhat prepared for negative possibilities, but you won't be ready for everything. However it will help you understand that there are things or situations which may result in disappointment. Hopefully you won't be quite so vulnerable and even fragile when faced with them directly, or afterward when the import of the occasion result sinks in.

There is no relief for sadness like there is for anger. Sadness and depression usually go hand-in-hand. So we need to eliminate one or the other (or both). Time usually works for sadness. But if you don't have time to pass, then the alternative is to "get happy". No, not through the use (or misuse) of drugs or alcohol. No, instead go for a walk or drive or visit an old friend. Physical exertion (walk, jog, bike, etc.) does the same thing as anger. It helps get rid of tension and hormones brought on by the sadness in the first place. Get a good night of sleep and see what the new day brings. If you are in a good mind state, it should be good.

So, after reading all of this, you know disappointment depression and sadness can be overcome. That is the final key. Now you know it is not permanent. Smile, a bit. It's a start.

That's all for now...

Good listening...Good feeling...

CH 6 : COPING WITH VIOLENT STUDENT DEATH

Coping with Violent Student Death

Almost every day, you can read a story in the paper, or online, about a student who was violently physically or sexually abused or killed, or all. Key to your reaction is it is sudden and unexpected.

This story of a victim, who was a 17 year old girl, is one such happenstance. An article in the Edmonton Journal called, "Calgary man pleads guilty to murdering 17-year-old stepdaughter" (Edmonton Journal – broken link), briefly describes the crime - as, what happened to Brittney McInnes.

This is extreme. It ended in death. There are many more violent attacks that do not and the psychological damage, and sometimes physical damage, will last forever. Sometimes the motive is robbery. Sometimes revenge. Sometimes there is no apparent reason at all.

A school yard robbery and bullying of an 11 year old child. He didn't want to return to school after the summer and killed himself on Labor Day weekend. The boy's name is Mitchell Wilson.

This story is of a 17 year old girl who was killed in a motor vehicle crash after the vehicle she was a passenger in left the road and collided with trees. The story from the CBC is here.

http://www.cbc.ca/news/canada/edmonton/story/2012/02
/13/edmonton-teen-killed-crash-court.html

A 10 year old girl was killed in a Jet Ski accident. An
update is here.

http://www.cbc.ca/news/canada/edmonton/story/2012/02
/15/bc-okanagan-lake-crash-edmonton.html

Emily Chaplin died in Okanogan Lake last summer.

Four different stories, but all kids. Death happens. But,
did it have to happen? What of those left behind?

Here is a story of a kid who was going to kill herself, but
didn't. This was a direct result of bullying. Here is the
CBC story of the suicide box, from her mother.

http://www.cbc.ca/news/canada/new-
brunswick/story/2012/02/16/nb-bully-victims-suicide-
box.html

How do we cope? Sometimes we don't. Not right away.
Shock and feelings of anger or denial or loss or other
reactions take place. Each person reacts differently. For
some it is devastating and mind-numbing. For others
who can rationalize the event and outcome and not be
moved by it, there is no coping needed as there is no
feeling, or response, at all. Most people fall somewhere
in between. Some people can limp along emotionally
until rescued and others cannot. So, how do we cope?
First, I think, by understanding. And then by accepting.
And then by helping others who are just going in circles.
These words are easy to say, but very hard to do.

Accepting the death of a young person is hard, especially for their friends and certainly for their siblings, parents and relatives. Again then, accept that it happened. This is not the time for blame, if any, or feeling of hate or ill will if the death was caused by another. This is accepting. This person who dies, a son or daughter, will not be heard again, except in the digital memories you already have. There will be great sadness. Sometimes so much so that there is no escape. Coping usually is done with the help of others who can help direct and guide you. Can you cope on your own? Sure, if you have to, but you may not like the result. Can you get over the loss? Not really. But you can, and must, accept it happened and think of the good times, the good memories. If the loss of a child was a result of a failure in a process or system or belief, then perhaps getting involved to effect change for the better would be really good for your mind and body. It would be a remembrance and celebration of life for others to share.

It was easy to say coping is hard. There is no easy answer to how do you cope because we all react differently. I believe the word, react, is the operative word. How do we react in our normal world? Well? Not so well?

Our guide to sudden death of a person so young and full of life is SHOCK. Shock because it is sudden, and unexpected. We can normally deal with expected and definite, say over a period of months due to a terminal illness, upcoming death. Shock is not a part of the reaction to a long term expected death. Now we know that we have to deal with shock. It can be massive. However it is usually quick as seconds, minutes or, at most, hours. If the reaction is longer than that then perhaps shock has given way to an overload. A mental overload can evoke physical reactions like collapse or passing out. A mental overload can be demonstrated by mind-wandering, refusal to accept or believe, deny it happened, and other life-altering reactions.

How do we cope? By dealing with shock first. We don't realize it is shock. But our first reaction is usually shock. It must be dealt with first. Then we can actually think and act, instead of just react.

So we start coping. The process, or experience, can go on for quite a long period of time, again depending on the person. Most people can not do it, heal or cope, alone. This is when you find out who your true friends are. Sometimes professional help is actually required. Please see my previous articles as well regarding help, and helpers.

I'll stop now...

Good talking...Good listening...

CH 6 : SADNESS: I DON'T WANT TO BE SAD ANYMORE

Sadness: I Don't Want to be Sad Anymore

I don't want to be sad anymore.

If you hear those words, you know the person saying it is in deep emotional trouble. Pain, even wincing sometimes - almost physical in nature. Help your child now. Before the pain becomes too great for them to bear. The phrase "I don't want to be sad anymore" is incredibly scary, especially if it is said more like a small statement and a sigh as well. Fortunately most kids don't get so depressed as to think of sadness as a darkness which never ends.

However Canadian girls seem to be much more troubled with emotional problems (usually not life-threatening) than boys. See the original release from Queens called, "Queen's-led national study identifies mental health as a primary concern for Canada's youth".

http://www.queensu.ca/news/articles/queens-led-national-study-identifies-mental-health-primary-concern-canadas-youth

So there we go. You have been compartmentalized. Easy and done. Well, no, not so fast.

What is it about reading something in the newspaper or online and not be affected by it or not even giving a very troubling story a second thought? Perhaps because we don't "feel" it. Or, we cannot put ourselves in the situation or life told. Or perhaps we just don't want to go there.

The story mentioned above should have been a wake-up call for any parent. The next time you walk down the street, look at the people coming your way. Look at the youngsters and see if they return your gaze, or look down or away. There are a lot of troubled kids in the world today, in every country and of every nationality. When you are troubled by something, that's what you think about. School, homework, studies, friends and parents are not at the top of the cognizant heap. That can mean skipping some classes and grades taking a nose-dive.

What can we do to help the kids who cannot overcome their negative feelings or their continuing despair? We can start be recognizing that the kids have feelings (surprise!) and that they are much more vulnerable than most adults. Sending a kid into a funk is easy. Try bringing them out of it. It is usually much easier to destroy than to build. Some people actually feel "good" when they destroy something. Some don't feel at all. However building, which takes much more time and energy and commitment, is usually much more rewarding and fulfilling. The same with people. If we help a kid, instead of tearing them down, then they stand a terrific chance of changing themselves, those around them, and possibly much more as well. We don't know how far the influence will travel but if we help it to be positive then the kid emanating it will have a good and beneficial feedback.

I'm sure that if you type "troubled youth" into a search engine, there would be millions of hits. Many results offering advice, guides, courses, schools, camps, etc. The point is that the kid, the boy or girl, has to get started by reaching out or initiating contact before it is too late. Sometimes a child may think no one cares because no one has ever helped them emotionally. So an attitude develops, which can be a "don't care" attitude. It can also lead to high-risk activities.

We can help a troubled kid if we have at least some idea what is on their mind. Sometimes it is something that just requires an explanation. Sometimes it is much more involved than that. A psychologist, due to their training, can usually zoom in on the troubling thoughts quite quickly. A parent isn't necessarily equipped to do the same. If a parent explains to the child that they will listen and assume a listening position, then the child might actually talk, and express by words or drawings or expressions in their own way, what is so troubling to them. Then help them. Do not criticize. Do not say things like, "if I were you...". Instead offer to help them arrive at a solution or explanation by working it out with them. Let it come from them, as much as possible. Act as a guide and mentor. Remember though, it is not about you as helper. It is about the child you are trying to help. Leave your stories out of it unless they directly pertain to the problem and use them as very brief examples to illustrate a point or option or alternative, etc. By actually listening and spending time with your boy or girl, you can be of more help than you could ever realize. Perhaps when they grow up, they will tell you. Always leave the 'they talk/you listen' option open, so that they KNOW that you will listen if they NEED to talk.

So, out of the millions of web pages about troubled kids who are sad, this is mine. I hope it helps you in a positive way.

Good listening...Good talking...

CH 6 : ARE YOU READY
FOR KIDS HELP PHONE?

<u>Are You Ready for Kids Help Phone?</u>

So many kids - so many problems. Kids from grade school to high school experience problems which affect their mental balance. It could be an exam, broken relationship, a mean parent, a bully, non-heterosexual. worrying, sleeplessness, parent breakup, death in the family or death of a close friend and the list can go on.

When you are troubled and are stuck, there is help available for you.

It is the <u>Kids Help Phone</u>.

<u>http://www.kidshelpphone.ca/</u>

There is a 24 hour toll-free number, but you can also post your issue or question in a forum. At all times you may remain anonymous. No one knows it's you calling or posting. Your post will be answered by a counselor. The phone will be answered by a trained counselor. Help is at your command. Just dial the number.

The following is from the Kids Help Phone website:

Kids Help Phone Promise
All calls we receive are anonymous and confidential.
Anonymous means that you don't have to tell us your:
* Name
* Phone number

* Address
We don't have caller ID, so we can't track your call.
Confidential means "in the vault." It's just between you
and the counselor, no matter what. Our service is about
helping you, not spreading your secrets around.

What is counseling?
Some people get a little weirded out when they hear the
word "counseling." That's okay. Basically, counseling
is about talking to someone who knows a lot about many
different issues that teens face. We think of counseling as
a conversation with someone who you can trust, who
won't judge you, and who wants to help.

Ready to talk? 1-800-668-6868
If you are not ready to talk, Ask Us Online might be the
place for you.

http://www.kidshelpphone.ca/Teens/AskUsOnline.aspx

Here is an article called, "Children feel hopelessness
when depressed",

http://www.cbc.ca/news/health/story/2011/05/20/kids-
help-phone-hope-tips.html

that appeared on the CBC website. It has stories and tips
for fostering hope from Kids Help Phone.

Good listening... good talking... good health...

CH 6 : TECHNOLOGY INDUCED ATTENTION DEFICIT SYNDROME

Technology Induced Attention Deficit Syndrome

TIADS - Technology Induced Attention Deficit Syndrome - *NEW*
ADD - Attention Deficit Disorder
ADHD - Attention Deficit Hyperactivity Disorder

Technology Induced Attention Deficit Syndrome is what I call the result of too many technology distractions, especially noticeable with kids. (Adults exhibit the same symptoms using some of the same technology and other distractions.) Examples of distractions are: texting, listening to an iPod or playing an online multi-player interactive computer game, or of course, doing them all at the same time. Then there is handheld net surfing and game-playing and calling on the cell phone. In the vehicle we should mention having a sip of coffee, watching the GPS and marveling at the heads-up car display and vehicle surround sound music system.

Some of the symptoms exhibited are the same as some of the symptoms of ADD or ADHD. For instance:

Predominantly inattentive type symptoms may include:

* Be easily distracted, miss details, forget things, and frequently switch from one activity to another
* Have difficulty focusing on one thing
* Become bored with a task after only a few minutes,

unless they are doing something enjoyable
* Not seem to listen when spoken to
* Daydream become easily confused, and move slowly

This particular problem is solvable without drugs or therapy. You could have a chat with the kids, which is easier said than done, and ensure they have time with people who are not "connected". Which begs the question, would they have anything in common? Actually, yes. Sports and swimming are two activities that come to mind right away. Getting a job is a good way to re-focus on other things.

There are other considerations as well. Going too far in the correction direction may result in withdrawal, depression, runaway or other activities not expected or intended. There is a balance which must be sought with a clear head. An objective and non-reactionary response seems to work best.

The big thing is that these activities are a mental phase, not a mental problem. After a few months interests change, sometimes replaced by other just as annoying distractions, and maturing is still taking place. Really, patience is the greatest virtue when dealing with TIADS.

Until the next time then,

Good teaching... Good learning...

CH 6 : STUDENT PERSONALITY DISORDERS – SCAPEGOAT THINKING?

<u>Student Personality Disorders - Scapegoat Thinking?</u>

I was going to write about Education Paradise Lost but then I realized very few people think of furthering their education as paradise.

Children manipulate adults. It is a given. How well they do depends on the adult. On the other hand, some kids do not know what is happening to them. Some know what is happening but do not know why, or how to stop. They actually do need help because they really cannot help themselves. However, there are those who are using something that cannot be measured, like a peculiar mental condition, as an excuse for poor behavior and other issues which may include laziness and the "I don't want to do that" attitude.

Here is a small list of 21st century student issues and resource sites.

List of children's disorders
"Official" childhood disorders (*and more coming all the time*):
http://www.nlm.nih.gov/medlineplus/childbehaviordisorders.html

Learning Disabilities in Children
http://www.helpguide.org/mental/learning_disabilities.ht

m

Children's Mental Health Resource List
http://www.nmha.org/go/children

Mental Illness in Children
http://www.medicinenet.com/mental_illness_in_children/article.htm

Mental Health Disorders - all ages
http://www.mental-health-matters.com/index.php?option=com_content&view=section&id=4&Itemid=27

Disabilities
http://www.buzzle.com/articles/disabilities/

A List of Psychological Disorders
http://psychology.about.com/od/psychotherapy/tp/list-of-psychological-disorders.htm

Good luck to us all with 21st century ailments and no solutions to speak of. Understanding the student is big. However, learning and understanding takes so much time and resources that the student becomes merely the test subject.

Well, universities need to output more shrinks. There are not enough now. The demand is outstripping supply.

What a world we live in today. I believe it will be a better world for most people, but not for some time. Meantime, we listen and learn and help occasionally, almost accidentally and unplanned.

Is it that so many people feel that other people should/must help them, instead of helping themselves? Perhaps. Is it that responsibility for oneself by oneself is something lost to/for this generation? Some blame their sorry state on anything or anyone, but never themselves of course.

Perhaps we should be spending much more time on developing self-awareness and self-help knowledge and skills. Well, we'll see.

Person use in Education is slowing down. Technology use in Education is speeding up. The gap is widening actually. This is not a situation which can/should/will continue. It must be addressed by our Education "consultants" who must stop thinking/responding like some government types.

Good learning...Good teaching...

CH 7 : HOSTAGE

A Student taken Hostage

If you are in the wrong place at the wrong time and are taken as a hostage, fear and resultant mental shutdown, or paralysis, can occur.

You haven't lived long enough to experience a full life but you've already lived long enough to experience death.

In a strange twist of fate, an American university student was killed when the officer trying to resolve a hostage stand-off killed her, as well as the hostage-taker.

The story on Fox news is here: Officer's split-second choice ended with Hofstra student, suspect dead after home-invasion

http://www.foxnews.com/us/2013/05/20/officer-split-second-choice-ended-with-hofstra-student-suspect-dead-after-home/

Apparently, according to the article, the student was being held in a head-lock. An officer looking at a target would have a clear head shot. Training for center of mass wouldn't apply this time. Confidence in accuracy would be paramount. Apparently eight shots were fired. To me, that sounds like panic. A double-tap to the head would have sufficed.

However, we are looking at student survival. You are

already a victim in this case. Let's try to make it temporary and come out of it alive and well.
So, what to do in this case while you are in a one-handed head-lock? Resolve panic. Think, you may die, and be done with that thought. Give yourself a chance when an opportunity presents itself. When the officer and hostage-taker aimed at each other, that is when to do the unexpected. Feign a faint. Drop as if you fainted and now the sudden weight will throw the hostage-taker off balance and let you go. As well, the effect opens up more of his body as a target. The hostage-taker may decide to shoot you for fainting and ruining his plan. Are you willing to take that chance?

There is no perfect world, or perfect plan. However it would be helpful for your survival, that you do something to help yourself survive if the opportunity presents itself. Once the panic is dealt with, resourcefulness can take over.

There is no easy solution sometimes. We can armchair quarterback all we want, but cannot change what is past. We can only learn from the past.

Perhaps, it was her time. But perhaps not for the next person in similar circumstances.

Hopefully you will be a survivor.

To quote the Vulcan greeting, "Live long and prosper"

PS: There are passive and active techniques to make someone let you go. The story above isn't a training tutorial. It is to open your eyes to possibilities for surviving an incredibly mind-numbing, out-of-your-control sudden situation.

CH 7 : DEATH: DEATH OF A CHILD

Death of a Child

I had to pass along this link and description of a narrative from a Funeral Director regarding the recent shooting deaths of 20 children and 6 adults at the Sandy Hook School in Newtown.

This is an unbelievable blog - in depth and very honest about feelings, parents, grief and children.

I warn you that it is brutally honest. After the loss of your child you, your family, your friends, students and even strangers you meet need help to come to terms with grief - and all its meaning and terrible effect. In his post he drives home the need for mental health help. You cannot do it alone.

http://www.calebwilde.com/category/death/children-and-grief/ - An Unimaginable Decision: A Funeral Director's Reflections on the Sandy Hook School Shooting (scroll about half-way down the page).

As well as honest, he appears to be very kind and caring.

Tell me, can a police officer be caring? If he or she wants to lose their sanity, yes. They are trained to keep their emotional distance. But even the officers who were first on scene at the school were not prepared for what they saw. It broke them down. They wept. It is my unfortunate prediction that most of them will not be in policing within a year.

Now, what about the parents, relatives, friends and acquaintances who are not trained for emotional disaster? They break down. The effects are long-lasting and deeply mentally injurious. For your sake, you must accept professional emotional help.

Heaven help you all - us all.

We are feeling too. Not your pain - no one but you can feel that. But pain none the less. We want to hope.

I can't go on right now...

CH 7 : DEATH: WHERE IS MY CHILD?

Where is My Child? Is my Child Safe Today?

Where is my child? Is my child safe today, this hour, this minute? You hear about a disaster with a school bus, mall or school and your child is there. Are they ok?

The worst feeling any parent can have is: the feeling in your heart and mind and soul when you don't know if your child is alive or dead.
The slaughter of the innocents took place on Friday the 14th of December 2012 - elementary school shooting, 20 kids are killed -
http://www.cbc.ca/news/world/story/2012/12/14/connect icut-school-shooting.html
Kids who were probably looking forward to the weekend, playing with friends, visiting relatives, getting ready to Christmas - not any more. Their peers are innocent no longer. So many, many people - kids, parents, and friends - mentally damaged in a heart-breaking way.

Or your child goes to school and is found choking to death by a lanyard he is wearing.

http://www.cbc.ca/news/canada/edmonton/story/2012/12 /14/calgary-bearspaw-school-district-accident.html

Further to my previous post about helping students after a disaster, here are some tips to help your kids after a specific event, such as the school shooting at an elementary school in Connecticut on Friday, the 14th.

http://www.cbc.ca/news/world/story/2012/12/15/connect icut-shooting-children-questions-parent-guide.html

There is no rhyme or reason, nothing that is predictable or makes any sense at the time. It happened.

Now you have to help your children make sense of it, because children NEED it to make sense, and understand it. You, the adult, need help too. Your reactions will greatly influence your children. Balance is the hardest thing to attain for you.

For you kids, understand what happened, be sad for the other kids and their parents if it overcomes you - and remember. Then start living again. It's ok for you to be happy again. It's ok to give your folks a hug out of the blue. The kids at the school didn't know if they were going to be killed or not. One student just wanted to go home for Christmas. Another student wanted to go home and give their mom a hug. Simple wishes and desires. Life, death and survival bring it all down to what is the most important thing in life. These kids got to go home.

Perhaps the most painful feelings for a child who attended that school are confusion and questioning and regret. Because you as a student at that school are alive and you sister was killed. Don't ask a question for which there is no answer. Please accept that you were chosen to live on, for whatever reason which may become clear in your future.

Be thankful for your life and celebrate the life of your

sibling. Soon this event will dull and not make you crazy sad. This is good. Let it happen. It is how we survive. We can remember without the numbing pain.

What a terrible loss...So many of us who didn't know the kids are saddened by their deaths at such a young age.

Some of the kids who were so close to it may be lost as well.

Parents! - Keep an eye on you kids! Sometimes thoughts of self-inflicted pain or death happen with kids exposed to such an incredible tragedy. Look for the signs.

There is no easy way to stop writing. There is so much that could still be said. I sincerely hope my post is helpful or beneficial.

...one for many

CH 7 : STUDENT DEATH AND THE FRENZY SYNDROME

Student Death and the Frenzy Syndrome

It's not unusual for news media to go after stories related to someone's violent death. Whether a car accident, stabbing downtown or suicide - it is news. If there are off-shoot stories, so much the better.

The Amanda Todd suicide story and related stories show no sign of abatement. Instead, it just gets worse. Now there is a story of the Alberta government's rehashed School Act (the Education Act) which has an anti-bullying clause, putting the onus on schools and students. The legislation will legalize a description of bullying. It will say what a student can and cannot do. It will say tattle on a perceived bully. Is there a 3rd party to listen or provide a hearing for any of this?
Here is an excerpt from the Edmonton Journal article referenced below, "*One of the significant changes in the Education Act, as introduced last winter, is that students would have the responsibility to "refrain from, report and not tolerate bullying," "whether or not it occurs within the school building, during the school day or by electronic means.""*.

All very nice and flowery. Students don't think or work that way, and they (for the most part) don't appreciate being legislated in this way. My prediction is that there will be very little cooperation.

We have talked about the use of legislation before. It is not the be all and end all answer. It is useful to press charges only.

What is useful is non-threatening education. Education not based on threat but instead on understanding. Many examples can be used in the classroom. How many times do I have to say it?
(Of course, that takes commitment - people and funds, well...)

Saying things about a person that are not complimentary is not hate. Putting every unkind word into a hate bucket is convenient and some people feel good because of it. They don't have to deal with it anymore. No. Deal with it. Saying something like, "Jimmy is wacko" is a kid comment usually said in jest. So try not to take a comment out of context.

Revisiting the still not changed School Act. Perhaps this fall it will be proclaimed. I hope that Education Minister Jeff Johnson revisits the act wording before the fall sitting of the legislature.

Don't get mixed up trying to define "bully". That was done a long time ago and is in criminal law as characteristics such as harassment, beat up (assault), injured, swarmed, and so on. The big difference today is that now bullying can be by remote control - timed and executed with the precision of an atomic clock. Anonymous. So a new definition of "bullying" is in order. Traditional bullying has been around for a very long time. Some in jest as in an older sibling harassing a younger sibling and mother saying something like, "Sally quit bullying your sister". This is not mean-spirited. It is just family kibitzing. However bullying in the school or workplace can be quite intimidating and very hard on the victim. It is not done in fun. It is personal, not using the internet. It is not remote-control. The new form of bullying is almost like 3rd party, like it's being relayed. This needs to be defined so that it can be dealt with.

Those who don't agree with popular feelings about someone are not evil or hateful. They simply don't agree and say why. Accusing a person of being "hateful" or saying "hateful things" is a convenient way of silencing opposition, negative (to you) comments, statements that disagree, or anything else a person doesn't like to hear. Good grief - get a life.

True bullies are easily identified and they are very few in number. Actual "hateful" comments are also very few.

It is amazing that a frenzy can still be stirred up these days based on innuendo. Not one solid example of "hateful" anything has been presented about Amanda Todd in the press. Bullying - yes - based on her own statements in her video.

Everyone needs to calm down and review the "facts". Learn. Suggest solutions or a way to address the identified issues or problems. Deal with it. Quit blaming it on the other guy. No more political gamesmanship over bullying-induced depression or suicide.

Ok, all kids get depressed at one time or another. They may say things they don't mean when they are depressed. Yes, it happens - a lot. Talk with the student about what was said but do it in a quiet friendly environment. You could start by saying something like, "did you really mean xxxx when you said it?" and go from there. Or start the conversation in any way that suits you and the student. A teacher in a school office probably won't go over well and usually nothing is forthcoming or addressed.

So, let's go over what are bullying words - they are just words - but used in a way that threatens or severely depresses another person to the point of self-injury, loss of self-esteem, loss of confidence, lost interest in school, lost interest in friends, lost interest in family. No interest in trying new things, quiet all the time or explosive outbursts, and more, always more.

It seems everyone who has ever said a negative comment is now broad-brushed in the bully category. That is like saying every boy with a necklace is gay. Wow. Crazy. Broad brush applied. No. Some people (VERY FEW) are bullies. The rest are not, even though they may say things like "who dressed you this morning?" or "I don't want to see you today" or "are you for real? - you're crazy!". Again, statements that simply disagree or josh are not bullying statements.

Let's get over the "everyone is a bully" thing and come back to earth.

Once the frenzy is over, hopefully common sense will again prevail. Well, one can hope.

Kids are supposed to live, not die - especially by their own hand. We must pay more attention and not ignore what we don't want to hear.

Try to learn from others, it usually doesn't hurt that way...

Update October 16, 2012
The frenzy continues and includes vigilante responses as well. Please see this Vancouver Sun page for much more...
http://www.vancouversun.com/news/topic.html?t=topic&q=Amanda+Todd
What happened to Amanda Todd should not have happened. In her memory let's try and fix the problem, not lay blame (let the police work on that so that an innocent person is not harmed during this crazy free-for-all).

CH 7 : DEAD – TOO LITTLE, TOO LATE

Dead - Too Little, Too Late

A teen killed herself a few days ago in B.C. She posted a video on Youtube stating, using written cards instead of voice, that she had endured bullying of all kinds and was getting depressed. She asked for help. SHE ASKED FOR HELP!

Help was not forthcoming. People know about the plea for help. Even her school knew about it before her suicide. They advised in a CBC article that they made resources available. Too little - too late. She was dead about a month after posting the video.

The story of Amanda Todd is mostly third party reporting, posts and hearsay. The only people who have any hope of understanding what happened and what lead up to it, would be her family, maybe, and the police as they pursue their investigation.

In the meantime, Amanda is dead. Let it be. Let her be. It matters not whether she was good or bad or misunderstood or anything else really. It is over.

Now lessons and learning begins. Oh, there are many people coming out of the woodwork saying this and that. There are knee-jerk reactions, based on what? Give it time. First, what happened and why? Not what we surmise or suppose, but what really was the cause?

I have mentioned several times in posts here that the

person who is depressed and considering suicide should ask for help. That is the hardest thing to do.
Well Amanda did ask. She was let down by the living.

Here is a link to the CBC article called, B.C. girl's suicide foreshadowed by video.

http://www.cbc.ca/news/canada/british-columbia/story/2012/10/11/bc-maple-ridge-suicide.html

Notice the picture taken from the video which says, on a flash card,
*"I have nobody
I need someone"*

Sounds familiar doesn't it? Almost the same words in other videos and notes left by the dead.

Here is a link to a CBC article called, What parents can do to stop cyberbullying.

http://www.cbc.ca/news/canada/story/2012/10/12/cyberbullying-strategies-parents-q-a.html

http://www.cbc.ca/news/canada/british-columbia/story/2012/10/11/bc-maple-ridge-suicide.html

From the article, this excerpt:
"Alexis Moore, author of A Parent's Guide to Cyberstalking and Cyberbullying, says that stories like these happen far too often. She spoke with CBC News about what parents can do to navigate the dark world of online bullying."

I talked with teens who did not know her and don't live

in the same province. Their insight is remarkable (if only we would listen). After discussing what appeared on the internet and what is appearing now, an insight into cyberbullying was mentioned. It is perhaps the most important item of all of our conversations. It was an explanation.

Three things were brought out:
Comments attributed as cyberbullying are quite often not originating in North America and are not seen as bullying at all.
Consequences are not considered at all, especially by students.
Words.

Someone writing on a wall or comment page or some other way of leaving a note, is writing words. There is no meaning behind them. They are just words.
To the person on the receiving end - they are not just words, they are innuendo, rude, harsh, depressing... the words affect the person.

I was informed that the third item is why cyberbullying will never go away. For the person saying them, they are just words.

There was an expression back in the old days:
Sticks and stones may break my bones, but words will never hurt me.
Well, they didn't have the internet or cell phones back then either. Words were said face to face.

Not anymore. Now it's anonymous.

Where do we go from here? Education is the step to take. Words can hurt. That is the message. Put that in the lesson plan.

Teens seem to be in a constant battle with themselves. They don't need any outside influence - it throws their balance off. Then euphoria or depression ensues.

Kids, pay attention to each other. You may save a life. Without being a policeman, firefighter or paramedic, you can save a life. Now - that is worth living for!

Good learning...good listening...good sharing...

Dr. Mike

CH 8 : ANXIETY

Anticipation Anxiety
(Added for this book edition)

These are my words from my experience and knowledge. I sincerely hope you find this article of value.

Many times kids don't want their parents to know they have been harmed, and they look for help elsewhere.

Kids and adolescents - try to talk with a parent first if possible. Parents - make time and listen without interruptions. Your child is most important now, not your friends.

Anticipatory anxiety is something every child and adult lives through, every day.
Occasionally though, it is so strong that fainting, or indeed a heart attack, can be the result. On the other side, suicide can be the result.

So, what is it? Well, it is thinking about what COULD happen to you and the physical response of your body. There is a probability as well. The "what could happen" is usually something bad, which will harm your mind, spirit or body. There are many put-down artists out there today. Try not to be one of them. Instead say something nice - what a difference. Bullying takes many forms and can be on-going, which causes anxiety for the bullied. The anxiety buildup can cause death. Be aware. This is NOT a video game. Tell someone you trust.

If you anticipate something happening to you and you don't know exactly what it will be, but it will be bad or make you feel really low and down and sad, then your anxiety level will increase as the passage of time brings you closer to the "event". Your heart will be pounding in your chest and you heartbeat becoming irregular as well, your skin color may change slightly and you will be on such an edge that when it is over you may collapse. However at the peak of anticipatory anxiety, you can suffer a heart attack, or harm yourself.

You usually cannot stop the anxiety, but you could think of options and strategies ahead of time, to develop and follow once the "event" has taken place.

This will actually help lessen the buildup of adrenalin and resultant want to hit something or run or scream or die.

Fear of the "unknown" is less threatening than the picked-on fear.

Some people fight back by being a "better" bully to the original bully. And it seems like it never ends. Once the power is felt, it is hard to let it go, or channel it into positive results.

On the probability side, if XXXXX the Bully waits for you around the corner every morning, then the probability is very high he or she is there again today - increasing you anxiety.

Are there any options available to you? You could take a different route. You could ride a bike. You could learn to fight. You could wait for him or her instead. You could tell parents. You could move. You could not go out anymore.

You could, you could, you could.

Ok, what possible solution is the best for you? Or, what would help mitigate the confrontation and its effect?

Don't get caught in a thought-trap. Fear and the resultant anxiety can paralyze thinking, but not feeling.

Anticipation can be really good for the right reasons like a holiday or going swimming or skiing, or something you really like to do and look forward to doing it.

So there is the good and the bad anticipation. Let's limit the effect of the bad. The next time you think of something bad because you just happen to think about it or there was a trigger event like a text message or post on a social media site, then you might try saying to yourself, what can I do about it? - And there WILL be something that can be done.

Get out of the victim mentality. You are not a victim. You are, just for now, being picked on. If you respond as a victim, it probably won't stop. Fighting back with words and otherwise can go a long way to shifting the focus of the bullies to another person from you.

That is the rub though - there is always another person, because bullies NEED someone to boss, lord over, pick on, denigrate, to make sad and more, so that they feel good themselves. It is usually a power trip.

Take the power away. Make it meaningless. Laugh at the bully whenever you get the chance - really laugh hard. You may get a punch but they won't "understand". It confuses them. If there is an idiotic text message, copy it or take a pic of it or save it (for parents/police later) and report it on your controlled social media page, with your comments showing just how stupid the bully really is. It will stop very quickly. Bullies love to embarrass others but hate to be embarrassed themselves. They "lose face".

Can you fight back? YES!

Do it nicely but with strength and determination.

Once the determination not to be a victim any longer is perceived, you won't be the victim any longer.

Another way to get the bullies off your back, is to get their respect. One way to do that is to become very good at something, playing an instrument, or dance, or math or science or computers or something you really like and can study. People respect those who are really, really good at something, even public speaking. Please think about it. It can be a great way to avoid physical violence and gain admiration at the same time.

Is there more to say? Well, yes - there are a great many books on the subject. Really though, what are you going to do to save yourself? That is, your sanity. You can involve others to help you. Try not to get stuck in time-shifting activities like smart phone games or "social" media site postings or the like for long periods of time. That is simply avoidance. The problem thoughts are delayed instead of fixing the problem(s).

Sometimes, even though you have family around you, it can seem that nobody wants you and that you have nobody. Usually, the "I have nobody" is really a missing best friend. A best friend who will just like you for you. How aloof are you? Do you actually let someone get close enough to you to be your best friend?

Thinking begets action - of some kind, but action none the less. Now let's try to make it positive for you, and by association, others as well.

Dwelling on an anxiety-causing problem is not an answer. It usually just makes you more depressed. Talking it out with sympathetic friends may help for the short term. However, a long term solution is really needed. So what is it to be?

To be brutally frank, if it is being physically bullied, I would put my battle armor on (figuratively speaking) and especially my game face, and go for a battle. Just the look of a "game face" can scare the biggest bully. The "game face" is the card and be prepared to back it up by the stare, and possibly, the walk. If you feel intimidated you will back up. Do not back up because, remember, you are NOT intimidated! It shows you are ready for anything and will take him or her down at all costs. That is scary.

If it is psychological bullying in person or by phone or

by text then try no answer or one syllable answers like, yes (yup) or no. Don't give the other party anything. And remember, the look to give them: the look of pity - for them, the look of no understanding, the look of no emotion at all; no smile, no frown, no anything. This is the best part - if it is in person, then drop something and slowly and deliberately walk towards them and make eye contact. If it is a group, walk towards the mouthy one or the biggest one. If they don't give way, get your face with a couple of inches of theirs. Then smile hard (just with the mouth, not the eyes). Back up one step and put out your hand for a handshake, never losing the eye contact. A true bully won't shake. They will just plan to "get even" later, behind your back. Why later? Because you called their bluff.

Shock is the best defence and the best offence.

If the bullying is through the use of "social" media, then another treat is in store for them. First, they are stupid. Second they have no idea that they can be tracked down. Third play a different game - a game you control. For instance, if they post something derogatory about you on a site, save it for evidence that can be used later, and perhaps, create an account on a different site and re-butte the comment, referencing the idiot(s) doing the original posting. Keep rotating your clean and pity-type comments from surprise site to site without leaving them time to catch up. There will be a whirlwind of activity and then nothing. My, my - it will stop. Make sure you don't start it again.

I have talked a lot about bullying because most

anticipatory anxiety is due to some form of bullying. Bullying-induced anxiety. But what if it isn't?

You have just finished high school? Now what? No money - no job - no income...

Or you had a job and were let go. Or you had a car accident and now you have no car to get you around. Or your rent is due and you cannot pay it. Or winter is coming and sleeping on a park bench is not so enticing anymore. Or, you were beaten up and when you leave the hospital, you know they are going to beat you up again.

Sometimes for some people, it is just the act of trying to get through each day. The stress can be so great without learned or earned coping skills, that suicide results. And then people say "why?".

And now we come back to opening up to someone. Even a stranger. Say out loud what it is that is driving you nuts, or into such a depression. You need to hear you as well.

Then listen - to your heart - your mind - and possibly the person you confided in.

Now the bad...

Sometimes the anxiety can not be shut off so easily and to dull the pain and memory, too much drink or drugs or all is done, just to forget for a little while. That may work, for a little while, so you do it again - and again, and again. Now you are a mess, and actually no one wants to be around you anymore. There is no love here, just pity and self-pity that only leads to one result - total despair. And, not caring any more. You go to jail and get dried out and punched out and you do it all over again when you can.

Now indeed you are going in circles. You need someone to help you. There are many resources to help, many people. But they cannot help unless you let them help. Encourage them to help. One step at a time. It can be done. Do you want it? Do you want to be free again?

Release the anxiety. Oh, I know that when you "don't care", there is no anxiety. Yes, there is. When you are fully awake and not under the influence, try releasing the anxiety. Hmmm - don't remember what is was? Then time to step up and step out. Ask the one who helped you for a helping hand.

Ok then, to the positive!

You CAN change! You CAN feel better! You CAN "handle" anxiety! Ok, let's figure out how this can be done.

Well first, identify the problem. If there is more than one, one at a time only. Identify the issues, you, you reaction, other people, objects, time - in other words, look at the whole picture. Now, identify a weakness, or strategy or plan that doesn't have to be direct. It can be indirect. Well that's good but let's go back to the beginning.

Who are you? Why are you here? What do you do?

What do you think? Do you have friends? Do you live alone? Are you a child or teen or adult by age? Are you a child emotionally? Do you exhibit any symptoms or behaviours that could be associated with a recognized "disorder"? Do people easily control you, your thoughts and body? Are you creative? What is the last thing you remember about your childhood? Do you remember your childhood at all? Are you an adult living with your parents? Do you watch a lot of "TV" or do you do a lot of game play or role play? Do you like music? Do you go out at night? Do you go hiking in the woods? Do you ride a bicycle? Do you own a motorcycle? Do you run or jog? Do you swim? Do you workout at a gym or fitness class? Do you beat people up?

No we are not building a psych profile. We are building a mental self-profile to where the highs and lows are each day. This will help to adjust the activity during a daily period to de-emphasize the lows and bring more attention to the highs.

If that sounds right to you then perhaps try it. How? Well, start by writing down your lows and highs. That is, the time of day the surroundings, your thoughts, the anxiety of now, the feeling you have during the now, the environment you want to be in - that is, changed from now.

Yes, it takes a long time to write it and not nearly so long to say it one on one. However we do not have the luxury of personal communication. I have tried to write this for all ages. Now I am going to specialize with the pre-teen and teen age group.

Let's start with pre-teen kids. According to an old expression, the "age of reason" was 7 years old. For some kids it is much younger than that. However, there is nothing to prepare a youngster for the horror of parental abuse or abuse from a "friend", stranger or enemy. The enemy doesn't have any meaning yet!? The early age when reality rears its head is quite often so foreign, that a mental blackout occurs. No memory, no understanding, no laughter, no smile - an automaton to be used or abused again and again.

Recovery? Sure. Many visits for psychotherapy or a psychologist trying to help. But no change. Until, a friendly dog or pet is introduced to the child at the visit. Many, many times the pet will draw out the child, in a most noticeable way. A smile and small laugh at last. This is when the child is "safe". No more abuse.

Let's go to teens now. They have had time to be well scarred by their life events of terrible ferocity. This can be changed/helped more easily than the subtle terrors endured. How many teens suffer anxiety? All teens. For most it is not negative or long-lasting or debilitating. It is usually sudden and over. The long term anxiety is what can turn into an anxiety-induced depression which doesn't go away during waking hours - which is what starts the cycle of alcohol and drugs use, and eventually abuse mentioned earlier. Not to mention, but I will, the self-abuse like cutting. A circle getting stronger and stronger - without a beginning or end anymore. That can be tough to break, interrupt or overcome. Yes it can be done.

WANT IT! Want what? Change - be better - FEEL better!

Sometimes friends have to be dropped and find new friends after your life-style change. Sometimes a move to a new city will be very helpful after deciding to change. Remember though, a new city has the same temptations you have already succumbed to in the city you live in now. If you change your city, it should follow that your life-style is changing too.

There is another side as well. You mat WANT something (or someone) so badly that you think about it constantly and dream of the possibilities, in anticipation of the actual event or being in the company of the person of interest. Sweaty palms are usually a good sign of anticipatory anxiety. This type of anxiety, although for a happy reason, still takes its toll on your body. You will probably need to give yourself more energy to accommodate the physiological response.

Negative symptoms noticed:

eyes darting about

nervous

fidgety

depressed

toss and turn sleep

eats too much

eats too little

cuts

aggressive

inattentive

doesn't answer quietly-asked questions

trust no one

doesn't want to talk

Positive symptoms noticed:

happy

inattentive

start a conversation and doesn't finish a sentence

talks more quickly than normal

wonders...about a lot of things (clothes to wear,
perception, likeability, etc)

clutches clothing in front of tummy once in a while

long sighs

smiles a lot

wants to talk

Both types of anxiety have the adrenaline effect of the
fight or flight response. This manifests as; easily

spooked or surprised, accelerated heart rate, thoughts (mind) racing, confused direction, time too fast/too slow, usually needs to "do" something active.

Dealing with anxiety. First, everyone reacts and responds to an anxious thought or input differently. If you have been trained to deal with certain anxiety-producing events like a vehicle collision or fire, then there is little or no anxiety. You do your job. However, if the event is outside your experience and knowledge, then anxiety can occur.

There is chronic (long term) and acute (short term) anxiety. Acute anxiety is usually high adrenaline, high action, high energy, fast thought, fast paced, reactive, and not thinking of ramifications during the event, and, still needs to work off the body high after the event is over. Chronic anxiety is lower paced, elevated heart rate, energy-consuming, seemingly constant low level adrenaline reaction and wearing the body and mind down.

Either type of anxiety is not good for you if too often or too long.

In summary then, deal with the stressors (the items - thoughts - which are causing the anticipatory anxiety). The anxiety can be dealt with by prescription drugs or alcohol or street drugs or sleep. However that solution is just treating, or dealing with, the symptoms - the heart-rate, the mind-numb, etc.

Go back to the cause. Deal with the cause - one step at a

time.

Anxiety can cause panic. If you think in small steps, there is much less panic, and a sense of I can do this (or overcome this).

Panic is mind-numbing. Panic due to physical and mental bullying is shock. Learn how to deal with a physical bully. Learn how to deal with the bully who tortures you mentally. There are ways and I'm sure that after a read of the articles here some alternatives have already presented themselves.

The biggest thing to overcome is fear. To stop being afraid. If you are not afraid you can usually deal with anything, because you are not powerless anymore.

The fear is within you. The cause may be external, but the fear is in you. Again, go back to - why. Identify why. Then try to figure out a strategy (a game plan) to deal with it. It may be a multi-part strategy and that's ok. (I'll do this, then I'll do that, and after that I'll do this, etc.)

Usually the only block now is - doing it. Making it happen. We talked about mind-numbing, paralytic fear. No more. Sometimes the fear of fear comes up.

You have come up with a plan, you feel good about it, you've covered all the bases that you know about and now is the time to release the fear, by action.

This article has covered a lot of territory in short order. I hope it wasn't too short and that enough was said to actually help.

CH 9 : CRITICAL THINKING 1

<u>Critical Thinking</u>

There seems to be a whole new emphasis on "critical thinking". What is critical thinking? Well, to quote Wikipedia - ok, the explanation is so long it cannot be quoted. You can read it <u>here</u> though.

<u>http://en.wikipedia.org/wiki/Critical_thinking</u>

An organization called, <u>The Foundation and Center for Critical Thinking</u> is an interesting resource.

<u>http://www.criticalthinking.org/</u>

Unfortunately there is no clear cut definition of "critical thinking" there. There is talk of concepts though. Then they go on to ask, "Why Critical Thinking?".

"Critical Thinking" appears to be another hobby horse or band-wagon that people are jumping on, without a clear understanding of what it is.
Teachers are saying, oh yes, we must teach critical thinking. Really. Just how are they doing that? Is each teacher interpreting guidelines and going from there? Is there any uniformity across schools? Are teachers using their own experiences or are they actually using government provided instructional materials? Do they interpret the materials and teach from the interpretation? Do they not critically think about the materials and teach using the materials as gospel?

An interesting exercise provided at the Foundation website involves the topic of Grammar. Learning grammar at a young age hasn't changed, but learning grammar from literature is mentioned. You can go here for the actual model being illustrated.

http://www.criticalthinking.org/resources/k12/TRK12-remodelled-lesson-6-9.cfm#266

The basics of thinking of any subject really hasn't changed much over the years. It seems that investigation, analysis, critique, problem-solving, summation and reporting have a new wrapper called critical thinking.

Oh I know, critical thinking proponents believe that critical thinking implies a host of attributes, and I quote from the Foundation website:
"Critical thinking is the intellectually disciplined process of actively and skillfully conceptualizing, applying, analyzing, synthesizing, and/or evaluating information gathered from, or generated by, observation, experience, reflection, reasoning, or communication, as a guide to belief and action. In its exemplary form, it is based on universal intellectual values that transcend subject matter divisions: clarity, accuracy, precision, consistency, relevance, sound evidence, good reasons, depth, breadth, and fairness..."

Also from the Foundation website, dimensions of critical thinking:

1. The analysis of thought
2. The assessment of thought

3. The dispositions of thought
4. The skills and abilities of thought
5. The obstacles or barriers to critical thought

I would like to be shown just one teacher who can teach these points.

Instead, let's start small with role-specific critical thinking. But before we do, Saskatchewan Education defines critical thinking better than anything else I've found.
The article is called <u>Critical and Creative Thinking</u>.
(dead link)
They include Creative Thinking as part of the whole. Brilliant!
Their definition is: *"Critical and Creative Thinking can be described as qualities of good thinking processes and as types of thinking. Creative thinking is generally considered to be involved with the creation or generation of ideas, processes, experiences or objects; critical thinking is concerned with their evaluation."*

Going back to role-specific critical thinking, it is explained very well in the same article, *"While critical and creative thinking may contain some common elements, they also take unique forms in unique areas of study. For example, critical thinking in mathematics does not necessarily involve the same mixture of knowledge, skills and processes as critical thinking in social studies or the arts. The criteria for good critical or creative thought in an area of knowledge depends upon the methods developed in that area for establishing the truth of its claims. This implies, then, that being able*

to think critically about literature is no guarantee that one will also be capable of critical and creative reflection using the concepts and principles of algebra as subject matter..."
There is much more there of course and I believe the article is a very important forward-thinking concept.

Here is more from Canadian sources:

How the Teacher's Role is Changing very good short brief

http://members.shaw.ca/priscillatheroux/teacherrole.html

Many links here: Educational Theory and cooperative learning

http://members.shaw.ca/priscillatheroux/philosophylinks.html

And, because not all kids learn the same way, Learning Styles, Modalities and Strategies

http://members.shaw.ca/priscillatheroux/styles.html

You will probably notice that some of the links above are all on one website, that of Priscilla Theroux, a Teacher in Alberta. Here is a link to her home page. There is much more to see there for teachers.

http://members.shaw.ca/priscillatheroux/index.htm

There used to be an old saw about newspapers, "you can only believe half of what you read". The internet is worse.

There are millions of websites to browse in your search for "critical thinking", however there is a lot of junk there too. Be careful, think while browsing.

CH 9 : CRITICAL THINKING 2

<u>Critical Thinking</u>

Today I read a long explanation of Critical Thinking by Steven D. Schafersman called, <u>Introduction to Critical Thinking</u>. It was published in January, 1991. An excerpt from his manual states, *"Children are not born with the power to think critically, nor do they develop this ability naturally beyond survival-level thinking. Critical thinking is a learned ability that must be taught. Most individuals never learn it"*.

The manual covers the following topics:

Introduction to Critical Thinking
Purpose and Rationale of Teaching Critical Thinking
Definition of Critical Thinking
Relationship of Critical Thinking to the Scientific Method
Formal Critical Thinking Programs
Course Areas In Which to Emphasize Critical Thinking
Critical Thinking Teaching Strategies and Classroom Techniques

The manual is written in layman's terms and is a very good read. The author doesn't discriminate, preach or cast stones. Critical thinking is explained, with examples, in a very easy to grasp way.

However, my research has found many converts who aren't quite so open-minded or generous. I find it interesting that many "modern" educators and organizations are recommending "critical thinking" as the be all and end all of teaching in the 21st century. Some label non-critical thinkers (how is that determined) as black and white thinkers, egotists and believe "non-critical thinkers" use "their" or "I", because they are selfish. The "critical thinking" proponents seem to be taking a really good evolved concept and turning it into another "religion", complete with converts and fervor. Get a grip.

Use "critical thinking" to explore critical thinking. Remember, rely on reason rather than emotion and keep an open mind.

CH 9 : CRITICAL THINKING – 3
HOW MANY DEFINITIONS NOW?

Critical Thinking - how many definitions now? –

How many definitions are there for the term: critical thinking?

Well, if you use Google and type: define: critical thinking in the search box, you will see at the top of the page, a link (Web definitions for Critical thinking) which will take you to several different website links, each with a different definition. As well, on that first Google results page and the following pages, there are so many websites promoting their own definition that one could be led astray for hours and days. Wow.

You know, for something that has been around for more than 60 years, one would think that the pundits would have an agreed-upon definition worked out by now. But no, some of the groups/organizations think that their definition is the one true definition. Good grief. Sounds like a religion!

Since there is so much disparity, then we must fall back to common sense (what!) and make a definition based on need, future education goals and the instruments to get us there.

One site that has a definition that I personally could work with, is from Prof. Brad Dowden at California State University. He has a light-hearted page with a definition

http://www.csus.edu/indiv/d/dowdenb/4/ct-def/def-of-ct.htm

which he likes which is actually a page of his Critical Thinking course. Be sure to read the Specific Skills page too.

A quote from his page:

"The following is a brief, but excellent, definition of "critical thinking" from a bill in the California State Senate that was trying to update the State's Education code:

Critical thinking is the ability to engage in reasoned discourse with intellectual standards such as clarity, accuracy, precision, and logic, and to use analytic skills with a fundamental value orientation that emphasizes intellectual humility, intellectual integrity, and fair-mindedness."

OK then, let's go to a so serious you can't crack a smile definition found here.

http://www.ericdigests.org/1992-2/critical.htm

"Paul (1992, p. 9-10) defines critical thinking as "disciplined, self-directed thinking that exemplifies the perfections of thinking appropriate to a particular mode or domain of thought." Glock (1987, p. 9) offers the following broad definition: "Critical thinking skills are (a) those diverse cognitive processes and associated attitudes, (b) critical to intelligent action, (c) in diverse situations and fields, (d) that can be improved by

instruction or conscious effort."

Then there is this more mellow, thoughtful <u>reference</u> to related "Reflected Thinking".

<u>http://faculty.ed.uiuc.edu/rhennis/SSConcCTApr3.html</u>

There are more "definitions" <u>here</u>.

<u>http://austhink.com/critical/pages/definitions.html</u>

So the beat goes on...

It is my hope that Alberta Education will present a coherent, logical, simple, easy to understand, easy to adopt, definition of "critical thinking", which will take us into the "21st century". The term has been bandied about quite a bit over the last 2-3 years in Alberta. I'm betting that for every school in Alberta there is a unique definition.

To think forward we sometimes have to look at the past, and preferably not make the same mistakes again.

Good teaching...Good learning...

CH 9 : MORE ON CRITICAL THINKING PART 4

More on Critical Thinking

There are thousands, or more likely hundreds of thousands, of online resources regarding critical thinking. There are different ways to learn and use critical thinking, depending on the discipline. The definition of critical thinking seems to depend on the discipline, the school, the department, the class, the country and so on.

This military site has a fascinating description and approach for the use of critical thinking in the Air Force. This page, "DEVELOPING THINKING SKILLS: CRITICAL THINKING AT THE ARMY MANAGEMENT STAFF COLLEGE",

http://www.au.af.mil/au/awc/awcgate/army/critical/roy.htm

which is referenced from this page, "Creativity, Thinking Skills, Critical Thinking, Problem solving, Decision making, innovation",

http://www.au.af.mil/au/awc/awcgate/awc-thkg.htm#critical

is a good read. This is just one of the many resources at Air University, the intellectual and leadership center of the Air Force (US).

The State of California appears to be leading the way for students with this site, "California Critical Thinking Skills Test",

http://www.insightassessment.com/test-cctst.html

which has many references from that page. It is based on what "*became known as "the Delphi Report," a document which continues to influence critical thinking theory, teaching, and assessment in the full spectrum of academic disciplines and professional fields*". More about this Expert Consensus on Critical Thinking can be found here.

http://www.insightassessment.com/9dex.html

Although this report seems to contradict my statement in the first paragraph, I'll go with my statement. Why? Not everyone/organization agrees - so we still have multiple "definitions" of "critical thinking"

Ok, on to a slightly different but related topic. This involves teaching and understanding a technique for fast critical thinking and conflict management. This site uses an Awareness Wheel to help people help themselves. The blog page called, "What Goes Around Comes Around: Keep practice communication on track with the Awareness Wheel"

http://www.pathwayscoaching.net/blog-articles/2009/11/20/what-goes-around-comes-around-keep-practice-communication-on.html

explains it quite nicely.

There are "different" versions of an "awareness wheel", some more detailed than others, but the concept seems the same. That is, the outcome.

It seems awareness/resolution/conflict/option/ "wheels" are common for a number of quite different reasons. This one is student/school related. Have a look at this "Conflict Resolution" page,

http://www.intime.uni.edu/citizenship/themes/single_themes/conflict_resolution.htm

 and also the Conflict Resolution Wheel

http://www.intime.uni.edu/citizenship/themes/single_themes/conflict_resolution/conflict_resolution_wheel.htm

For elementary school students. The Conflict Resolution Guidebook is linked from the initial page to a pdf file.

I recently attended a two day Critical Thinking workshop and I must admit that I had no idea what would be presented, as the attendees were corporate clients. It was a learning experience instead of just a what-it-is lecture. It was quite a valuable learning and doing exercise and the instructor/facilitator included maximum use of an "awareness wheel". Other techniques were discussed and used and some of the material was influenced by authors such as, Stephen Brookfield, Marilyn Herasymowych, Henry Senko and Edward de Bono. Thank you E.

Good luck...Good teaching...Good learning...

Dr. Mike

CH 10 : RAISING KIDS

Raising Kids - Excerpt 1

Excerpt 1 from Raising Kids - the Old and the New.

Raising kids today is nowhere near the same as it was one or two generations ago. You could write several books about it.

Quite often these days a child day care is involved from an early age because both parents work. Or it could be a single parent who is working. Most families in middle-class North America were single income earners not so long ago. Inflation hadn't hit yet. The mothers usually stayed home and raised their kids. There was no need for a day care. Once the child was old enough for kindergarten, they were usually enrolled and would spend a half day there for four or five days a week. Then grade one and formal schooling was underway. The child went home after school to the welcoming arms of their mother, most of the time. Of course fathers were involved but usually in a more administrative role.

How things have changed since then. The norm seems to be working mothers and fathers, day care and pick up after work. Home in time for supper, usually. Kids are cranky and so are the parents. It's quite a job of conscious willing in order to have a harmonious family relationship each day.

I was talking with a boy in his late teens the other day. We were talking about his knee injuries and how susceptible he is to injury.

We talked about other kids we knew who also suffer from being injured easily or who have ligament or tendon issues. He thought it had to do with the diet and food available today. Kids of yesteryear were not subject to being easily injured and were of a thicker, sturdier build instead of the mostly slender kids of today.

So perhaps it is both diet and nurturing. Mothers don't get a chance to nurture their kids much anymore, so tiny kids are left to their own devices. They are being fed and brought up during their most formative years by strangers. And we wonder why kids have so many problems, both mental and physical. Mental problems seem to abound.

Unfortunately, during this economic climate of uncorrected huge inflation since 1975, there seems to be no solution for a more personal raising of kids.

What can we do to help our kids recognize that the parents are the authority and most loving? Well, one could start by saying it every day. Most kids are not mind readers and need audible stimulation and reminders. But in this epoch of rush, rush, rush - it seems to be forgotten.

The new age seems to be kids with smart phones and gaming computers. Many kids seem to feel they really don't need parents, except to feed and clothe them and provide a roof over their heads of course. Parents are being used and they know it but, for the most part, don't know what to do about it. Kids are savvy about a lot of things, that is, sharing sites and the internet in general, however they are not too savvy about talking to others who are not their friends. Talking to adults seems to be so foreign to them that they really don't know how to act or respond. Kids today are wired to their phones. Kids of yesteryear were not wired to anything and because of that, they had a much more broad level of life experience than kids of today at the same age. Mind you, they did have sex, booze and rock and roll.

For good or bad, the dice is cast. All of us have to go with it because this time the present cannot be rolled back to the past, or the past merged to this logarithmically changing present.

So, what and how? Well, the rug has been pulled out from most adults. So the first thing is to find the balance again. Then we can go forward and try to get a handle on technology, which is like a runaway train at the moment. Unfortunately, for many, technology is replacing common sense thought and response. Both kids and adults are learning many new ways to be rude and obtuse by remote control. How do we get a handle on a return to civility and common sense? Oh, and there is a correlation between our new technology and what it allows a person to do and learn - and - the flawed mental processes which develop (because of it). The flawed mental state can be turned into a mental disease or condition or disorder or syndrome, or whatever else we want it to be. Sometimes convenient when we don't want to do things which take us away from playing with our toys, or interfacing with other people or going to

school...
We can look up symptoms on the internet and away we go.

However some people actually have mental or physical issues. Based on what? Upbringing, incest abuses, relationships, not wanted, sudden orphans, rape, loss of friends due to a move, accident, bullying, shyness, flash anger, physical problems (environmental, pregnancy, gene or chromosome related issues). These folks usually just want a normal life. It is hard to cope without help. Today there is help, and hope.

Thank goodness there is hope...

CH 10 : PAST TENSE

Past Tense

For the most part, we live just a hair from the past. We can see the past, feel it, smell it, touch it and be intimately aware of it. One thing we cannot do is change it. Sometimes we wish we could though.

We look around us and watch our present become the past hour by hour, minute by minute and second by second - and we don't give it a second thought. We are so wrapped up thinking we live the present. Well...

That leads us to the future of course. Well, it didn't have to, but we will say it does. Do we live in the future? Not really. Do we live for the future? Not really - most don't. Some folks do though. And we say how did they know that? Or, they seem so brilliant because they know so much and seem to see what's coming.

Every now and then (now and then - what a great phrase!) look forward - future-look. Now, perhaps you can do that already. Can you feel the future? Can you smell the future? Well, if the toast is still burning, yes. So, we should leave our old mind trappings by the side of the wall and accept our new perceptions. Wow, what a difference.

Sometimes the future is rushing at you like a locomotive on the tracks at 80 miles per hour, or perhaps like a summer thunderstorm. You can see it, hear it, feel it and respond to it (run, enjoy, or ?). You have a present tense response to a certain future event. How cool is that? Depends of course. Impending death or injury is not cool.

Now, what about a future event or thing you cannot see, smell, feel, taste or hear? It could then be a concept, a perception, a possible outcome, a possible event, a prediction, a value, an idea, a persuasion or something as simple as the outcome of a flip of a coin (which is not simple, but...).
So if we can conceptualize, we can see "into" the future. Perhaps our future or that of someone else. Ah, a concept is not a future unless it can come into being in some way.

An exercise then. Sit and relax with no distractions. Now think of what you are going to see, smell, etc. one minute from now. Then stretch that thought to one hour from now, then one day from now and then one week, one month and one year. This is your future you are looking at, as if from a looking glass in your mind.

Can you change your possible future? Yes. Doing so offers you a new, different future, which can also be changed or influenced. You don't need a looking glass or crystal ball for this. A single focus or clear mind will usually do.

Your future depends a great deal on your mental state, happy or sad, depressed or jubilant, etc. Of course, this is no surprise. Just thought I would actually say it.

So if we can affect our future, what do we really want in

our present?

Most folks don't know.

What do you want? Ok, back to the drawing board. No, we're not going to get into meta-physics here.

Let us look at past, present and future this way. Although many books have been written by philosophers, scientists, dreamers and many others, we will take the simplistic view. They are joined together. There is cause and effect. And most important, there is sleep. There is no delineation while sleeping and dreaming, or especially thinking while sleeping. When you go to sleep with a question, and wake up in the morning with the answer, you don't know how you got the answer, just that you have it - the answer - the solution. Where did it come from? We don't ask. We don't care. We don't know.

It is possible that for every question there is an answer? However it may not be answered yet, in our "time". If a known question has no answer and you want an answer badly enough, you will strive to find it, even if it take the efforts of many to do so.

Can you imagine it? Ah, that is the secret. If you cannot imagine the question, what is the answer?

If a solution "appears", what was the question?

Accidental invention happens quite frequently. So a question is developed so that the answer is accepted. There are quite a number of accidental out-of-the-box solutions, to questions we didn't know existed.

So out-of-the-box thinking is possible and, most important, I believe person-trainable.

However I am way off my original topic so now we go back there.

Let's use the example of decision points. Four directions per event. We can go forward, back, left or right. Each direction takes us to a new, not yet explored or visited, decision point. If we go right for instance, we will not experience the future related to going straight ahead or left or going back. We are on a new course which takes us to another new decision point and possible directions. I think it can be seen that our future is determined by many "decision points". Does that "cloud" or "confuse" the issue of seeing the future? No. You are seeing one of many what-if possible futures. People do what-if exercises every day. Businesses do it. So what-if the future is actually going on quite regularly. It can be seen as not some form of ritual, but more as a form of best guess (based on all available info) prediction. Even stock markets play into this.

However back to us or a single person, who wants to have at least some idea where he/she is going and how to get there. Well, it's time for you to best guess your future but, what input/info are you going to base it on? Hmmm, a thoughtful response in indicated. Form the question just before you drift off to sleep and "sleep on it". You may have your "answer" in the morning. If you do not, sleep on it again, and again. However asking the right question is important. Or perhaps asking the question the right way.

This will help you be more aware of your present, because you know how it came to be. As a result, your past will be rich and memorable and indeed, thought-provoking. So now we are back to the past. Can the events and knowledge of the past affect the future? Certainly.

There are some events we never want repeated and we will go to great lengths to avoid any repetition. This can apply to individuals, groups, organizations and governments.

Finally, past tense can be mixed with present thought for future tense events. Past tense matters.

Needless to say (I hope), this is my 2 cents. Your mileage may vary.

Good learning...good thinking...

CH 10 : TAKE ME SERIOUSLY

Teens ask - Take Me Seriously

Take me seriously - please! A simple plea. Not often vocalized. Look at the kid's eyes when they try to be. Not when they are laughing and having fun, but when they are body-quiet and soft-spoken.

Teens desperately want to be heard and listened to and not made fun of.

It doesn't happen often enough. We wonder why there is so much grief and despair. Wonder no more, adults are mostly the cause. The kids make a mistake and we often don't give them credit for good decisions.

The peers of teens can be a problem too and for some their behaviour is the same as that exhibited a hundred years ago. They still pick on each other and if you can't take it you withdraw and become a loner or an exile. Yes, it is still going on. The biggest difference from a hundred years ago is the absence of black eyes. There seems to be much more psychological damage nowadays. In the older days if you and another had a problem with each other, you would have a dust-up and be done with it. Now, you can harass each other all day, every day, without actually coming into contact at all. Welcome to the new "enlightened" age. This experience side-tracks kids into an emotional stasis. It is hard to be taken seriously when you don't say anything.

AS a kid, how do you get an adult to take you seriously?

Well, the one who teases you and makes fun of what you say or do probably won't unless they get a shock affecting their normal life and response to it. No, I'm not going to give you advice, just observations.

Kids who want to be taken seriously, want, and need, respect. These are kids adults can guide, and even teach - if they respect you.

The biggest challenge for adults is listening. Sometimes adults think kids don't listen. So the adult stops listening. Perhaps using a feedback mechanism to determine if the kid understood what you said (they did hear you) would be appropriate. Then when the teen tries their hand on a topic which is serious (important) for them, you will listen.

Try, as an adult, to get across to the teen that listening and being serious goes both ways.

Well, ok then. I see many kids who are so open and wanting for acceptance and appreciation and recognition that they are indeed very emotionally vulnerable. Adults must recognize that and be more cognizant of the teen's state of mind.

To the teen: Try not to wear your heart on your sleeve. Some people you know are not nice. Fortunately though, most are nice.

Well, back to "take me seriously". If you have the respect of others you will automatically be taken seriously. So really, respect is what must be earned, in order to be taken seriously. And that, you can do.

Where does respect come from? The Respect store?
Alas, no. Some people think respect can be bought.
Nope. Quite often they are laughed at, but not respected.
If you lead by good example, respect is earned. If you
follow in an exemplary manner, respect is earned. If you
become very good at something, respect is earned. If you
save a life, respect is earned. If you are earnest and
enthusiastic about something close to you, respect will
be earned.

There are many ways to earn respect. You are still
young, but nonetheless, start now. Even dressing well,
with flair, will earn respect. Yes, it can be done. Start
thinking about it. I believe you will find your way, and
be taken seriously when you need to be.

Learning for life...

CH 10 : ADEPT AT ADAPTING

Adept at Adapting

Learn well students - you will need it in our future. Most of all, be adept at adapting. It will become an essential skill.

Have a look at this excellent article called, "ARE YOU ADEPT AT ADAPTING?" by David Bowman.

http://www.ttgconsultants.com/articles/adapting.html

Here is an excerpt:
"May you live in interesting times," has been a toast offered to good friends for hundreds of years. However, never have times been more interesting than now.

Interesting, yes. Comfortable, perhaps no - at least for many of us - because today, the word "interesting" often is equivalent to the word "change." And, some are not comfortable with change.

Please read the rest of the article. Hopefully, it will give you hope and a possible plan for your future.

Good learning...Good reading...

CH 10 : LOST IN SCHOOLING

<u>Lost in Schooling</u>

Lost in Schooling - Special Education won't be able to keep up.

iPads are required for some courses at the University of Alberta.

Can the special Ed kid use it?

Can the special Ed kid go to university?

The province wants all kids to have the opportunity to complete grade 12, no matter how long it takes. That's good that they have the opportunity through special education, which is provided at most schools.

In Alberta, educating students with special education needs in inclusive settings is the first placement option to be considered by school boards in consultation with parents and, when appropriate, students.

Inclusion, by definition, refers not merely to setting but to specially designed instruction and support for students with special education needs in regular classrooms and neighbourhood schools.

This document outlines the requirements for school boards regarding the delivery of education programming and services to students with special education needs in grades 1–12. These requirements are organized into the following four areas:

* Access — students with special education needs are entitled to have access in a school year to an education program in accordance with the School Act . Students with special education needs receive adapted or modified programming that enables and improves learning.
* Appropriateness — educational programming and services are designed around the assessed needs of the student and are provided by qualified staff who are knowledgeable and skilled.
* Accountability — the obligation to answer for the execution of one's assigned responsibilities.
* Appeals — timely, fair and open processes protect the rights of students and parents and address differences of opinion about the education of students with special education needs.

Taken from the Standards for Special Education, Amended June 2004

For more information, read the complete Standards for Special Education document on Alberta Educations' website.

http://education.alberta.ca/media/311334/423.pdf

But, what comes after high school?

Good learning...

CH 10 : IMPRESSIONABLE STUDENTS-BE CAREFUL

<u>Impressionable Students - Be Careful</u>

Impressionable Students can be any students sometime in their career.

Here is a scary article (Edmonton Journal) showing just one target item. There are more.

It is from a <u>study by the RCMP</u>. It shows the con. Just like spear phishing emails. Anything to get to the kids and get them to respond. Basically attracting cannon fodder...

Here is a quote from the article:
A new RCMP report says extremist groups — from Muslim radicals to violent animal rights activists to white supremacists — are employing increasingly sophisticated multimedia tools to attract a young, computer-savvy generation of followers.

Please read and understand the message in the article. Some students are easily conned. Here is another quote from the article:
"Using bright colours and in some cases, illustrations stylized after children's cartoons that seem inspired by Disney and other leading companies, the websites are visually appealing and in contrast to the malicious content they contain," according to the report, Youth Online and at Risk: Radicalization Facilitated by the Internet.

Be careful out there. The internet is like the wilderness. You don't know what kind of animal is out there, but the animal is looking for you...

Good learning...try not to repeat the mistakes of others...

CH 10 : THE ART OF COMMUNICATION

The Art of Communication

Communication of any kind usually implies a conversation or dialogue with one person, or occasionally more than one person.

The art of personal communication is listening.

Now listening is good, but to do the person listened to justice, you must also suspend your own belief system, which includes judgement. You are not the other person. If you are going to listen to the other person, then don't believe they share your values at all. Just listen.

Most of the time a person just wants to talk, rant, know at least one other person has heard him/her, bounce ideas and solution thoughts off the listener and in so doing, release stress and tension and possibly achieve a positive result. However if the listener is not really listening, then there is no point and the person wanting to talk will probably never talk about anything serious with the listener again. This is more than disappointing for the person wanting to talk, it's depressing and leaves the person sad or frustrated as well.

Remember, active listening is the key to any communication between two people.

Attending behaviour

focus - topic - person

posture - mannerisms - eye contact

our own feelings and distracting thoughts

Listening
Communicated understanding

Good learning...Good teaching...

CH 10 : EDUCATION TODAY –
WHAT DOES IT MEAN?

Education today - what does it mean?

Well, it has been a while. I just finished another project and musing time is available again.

What does what mean? Ok-Ok Thinking about education and narrowing it down from global proportions to local proportions, I thought of that old expression, "getting an education" or some say "receiving an education". Back to that in a moment.

We "educate" ourselves all our lives. It seems that the learning doesn't really stop. The "formal" education may come to an end, but the daily informal education goes on and on. Many job descriptions say, under qualifications; university degree, certificate, or equivalent experience. Quite often, the life experience learning will out-shine what is learned by getting a degree. Oh, a degree is good to have. Do try and get scholarships to pay for it though. The degree, and other qualifications, looks very good on a business card. I am reminded of a social worker I met many years ago. He had many qualifications listed on his business card; his bachelors, masters, doctorate and so on. At the end of the list was one more which was indicated by, "PaL". Hardly ever did anyone actually ask what it meant. It was an inside joke for him and it meant, "Psychotic at Large". This little story illustrates the point that many people think that the more qualifications the better, but don't take yourself too seriously. Probably no one else does. Many people think qualifications equal respect. But really, respect is earned - unless you're the boss perhaps.

Let's go back to "getting an education". Remember another expression, " I'll learn ya!"? Well then, perhaps we are not giving our kids an education, we are giving them a learning. They are receiving a learning. To me it makes sense but perhaps it doesn't make sense to others.

Something to think about though. If we give it too much thought, we might just change the way we teach a bit. After all, we are there to give our kids a learning, so that they "get a learning". Now, since all kids do not learn the same way or at the same time/speed, or using the same style, we can check their "learning" and, knowing they are "learning", we can adjust our teaching in order to "learn" them better. Heh Heh. Sounds a bit like a hillbilly, but perhaps in their direct way, they had the right idea.

Ok, do you remember how we "learned" many years ago? We learned by reading, listening and seeing. Reading, interpretation and demonstration/reinforcement. I'll leave this with you, is it still that way?

Good learning...

CH 10 : HAVE YOU BEEN TO TED.COM?

Have you been to TED.com?

For those of you who have not been to TED.COM it is a terrific place to see video talks of a vast variety of subjects, which can be inspiring, educational, courageous, funny, emotional, creative, and much more. This is a place where excellent speakers, who seem to really know their subject, enthusiastically bring the live audience into their world with thought-provoking presentations, delivered with style and humor.

This talk, Ken Robinson says schools kill creativity, is a fascinating talk, with humorous anecdotes, well worth the listening and the watching.
http://www.ted.com/talks/lang/eng/ken_robinson_says_schools_kill_creativity.html

There is much, much more at TED.com and you could be there for hours.

Have fun - good teaching - good learning...

CH 10 : MEET ME AT THE CORNER

Meet me at the Corner

You may wonder about the title of this blog post, but it is the title of a website for kids which has virtual field trips as video pod casts.

The description and links below are from the author, Donna W. Guthrie.

Directed at America's school children, each show explores the world and its wonders from a child's point of view. During each video pod cast a child host serves as tour guide, leading the viewer to historic and cultural sites. Each show includes a suggested reading list and a Learning Corner of follow-up activities for school children ages eight to twelve.

From the author, Donna W. Guthrie, "Our new episode on THE AMERICAN COWBOY features an interview with Bob Norris owner of the T Cross Ranch in Pueblo, Colorado. Mr. Norris talks about the history of the horse and his life as a modern-day cowboy. Our videos are posted on our website, Currki (http://www.curriki.org) and TeacherTube (http://www.teachertube.com)".

The main site is at www.meetmeatthecorner.org, where the videos are also hosted.

I visited the main site and found the videos short and well edited. Good learning.

CH 10 : HAND – EYE COORDINATION IN YOUNG STUDENTS

Hand - Eye Coordination in young Students

Sports and computer or handheld gaming help develop hand-eye coordination.

Specialized coordination between hand and eye is just part of what a modern kid is capable of doing. I was watching my son play World of Warcraft and his mastery of the intricacies of the game and addons was fun to watch. The screen has what seems like hundreds of icons for so many things, all of which he knows. So he carries on a text conversation, plays the game, checks accounts, checks players, checks his guild, his booty and much more, all at the same time, and quickly, as he explains what he is doing and showing me. Fascinating!

Kids can think multi-level without batting an eye. They are actually developing more of their brain at a younger age. (They are certainly getting taller as early teens as well.)

Where is it going from here? Ask any kid who doesn't need a calculator anymore in school because it's like a game. Oh, and the school system is falling a bit behind and many kids are bored.

This leads us back to 21st century schooling. What do we need to do to challenge the kids of today and tomorrow?

Perhaps the first thing to do is try and understand their capabilities, not from a clinical point of view, but a personal experience point of view. Let the kids show YOU! Take part. Unstructured. Oops, what, can't do unstructured? Well, the new teachers can, but they are not allowed to do so unless it is a "special" school.

Can kids learn better in a semi-structured environment?

CH 10 : FIGHT TRAINING FOR STUDENTS

Fight training for Students

It seems that students haven't really stopped getting into fights at school. But what is more prevalent is getting someone in the hall or playground. Nothing done as a fight or a pick-on, just surprising someone with a punch or jab, ostensibly playfully.

The kids with fight training seem to fare better as they can react quickly and return the favour. When the student who started it is on the receiving end of a quick and effective response, that is usually the end of it. It seems to be kids testing each other.

These days it is important that kids have defensive/offensive fight training. For instance, my son was waiting for a bus at a bus stop after school and a guy tried to physically move him down the street to what, we don't know. However my son dropped him, got on the bus just coming around the corner and that was that. We have always said the objective in a fight is to end it as quickly as possible, and that is what he does. His self-defense training gives him a lot of confidence. So the 6 years of karate pays off each day - just in self-assured awareness.

It is not so much the school kids who are trouble anymore, it is the predator driving or walking past looking to grab an unsuspecting kid like the one example above. It could be on a school day or weekend. Ordinary normal kids need new skills today - urban survival skills. Some kids who live a high-risk lifestyle already have the skills, but most kids do not.

As parents we think that the world environment is better and we are more kind and more thoughtful and our kids are too. Perhaps. But school age gangs try to recruit kids, perhaps your kid, with the lure of money or drugs, or perhaps by intimidation, and the road to a vicious and deliberately uncaring way of life and thought gets underway. Girls specifically are at risk as casual sex gives way to sex for goods and then blackmailed into much more than that.

There are many traps for kids these days which were not there two generations ago. Two generations ago kids were innocent. Not anymore. Not since the internet.

I believe we need to give our kids the tools to survive in the world of today and tomorrow. Now, that means online and gadget (iPod, etc.) safety and physical safety. So we educate the mind and educate the body.

These are tough times for parents. Most kids don't understand the dangers yet. What sets a kid up as a victim? Another blog is coming for that diatribe.

On a positive note, most parents are much more aware and keep a watchful eye on their kids and their friends.

I do hope that parents and kids have a great summer together.

CH 10 : KIDS, JOBS AND HIGH SCHOOL

Kids, Jobs and High School

Should kids have jobs in high school? Should kids be paid to go to high school?

Here is an article which goes into the subject a little more called, Should kids have jobs in high school?. A good argument is made for letting kids enjoy school and extra-curricular activities. But kids need money and parents usually have a problem of just giving kids money. So now we go to our second question, should kids be paid to go to high school? Well, here is the for and you'll find the against below.

http://www.blisstree.com/articles/should-kids-have-jobs-in-high-school-155/

Would get an education.
Wouldn't drop out of school.
Would attend classes.
Would take part in school activities and after school activities.
Wouldn't have to worry about money.
Would be accountable to parents for school progress.

Against:
Parent may believe the student wouldn't develop a good work ethic.
Student may not make enough money.
Student will miss some school activities.

There is much more of course and hopefully this will get you thinking and discussing it.

CH 10 : EYE CONTACT IN THE CLASSROOM

Eye Contact in the Classroom

Remember when teachers insisted that eye contact be maintained with all the students in the classroom? If a student was looking down (and not writing) or away, teachers felt that the student wasn't listening or paying attention. Then they would yell at the student or throw something at them. (Usually a chalk brush in the old days. I suppose in some schools it hasn't changed.)

Now we know that there are other reasons, such as, the teacher is boring, speaks in a monotone, turns their back to the students for most of the class with more attention on the board than the students, gives a class assignment for the period instead of teaching, is afraid of the students (and they can tell), doesn't want to be there (again, students can tell), is thinking of something else (distracted), is in a bad mood, wears weird clothes (distraction), yells at the students, speaks too softly, can't explain a concept, isn't prepared, fumbles around, commands no respect, doesn't challenge the students, or the student is too far away from the board and can't read it, or the student can't hear the teacher properly, or the student doesn't want to be there, or the student has a big worry (not all students come from a happy home life) and is distracted by it, or the student got harassed by another student earlier, and on and on and on...

If the student seems to be inattentive, perhaps the teacher

should make a private attempt to find out why.

A caring teacher at an elementary school did some fact-finding with a 10 year old student one day. The student was getting lower and lower marks as time went on. The teacher found that the student couldn't see the board, it was out-of-focus, fuzzy. The student needed glasses and the student and parents didn't realize it. The glasses made the difference and the student is an "A" student now. There is usually a reason. So let's not yell at the student, let's find out the "why".

Oh, the seemingly inattentive student? If they can hear fine, they are usually getting everything that is said. They are simply not acknowledging it by looking at the teacher.

CH 10 : HOW DO YOU INSPIRE?

How do you Inspire?

"How do you Inspire?" is a huge topic. I have chosen a number of sites to represent not only schools/students, but business as well. This is a topic which involves almost everyone in their daily lives.

From the UK we have this article by Dr Maggie Aderin-Pocock, who was inspired and wants to inspire a new generation of students. Her very good article called Let's inspire the next generation of scientists is well worth the read.

http://www.telegraph.co.uk/scienceandtechnology/49850 76/Lets-inspire-the-next-generation-of-scientists.html

A book called Inspire! by Lance H. K. Secretan, looks like it would be well worth reading. A write up about the book can be found here.

http://books.google.ca/books?id=dTYPCDJ9OwgC&dq =How+do+you+Inspire?&source=gbs_summary_s&cad =0

He looks at a corporate or business environment. An excerpt from the blurb, "...*The key to extraordinary long-term performance lies in a transformational commitment to inspiring people rather than motivating them...*"

And from the HR Cafe Blog a short article by Michael

Boyette called Motivating employees: How do you inspire workers?. Also a good read.

http://hrcafe.typepad.com/my_weblog/2009/03/motivating-employees-how-do-you-inspire-workers-.html

Well, here is a website representing a group of educators who care about 21st century skills and learning. There seems to be a huge emphasis on technology for developing 21st century skills. Perhaps this is due to the influence of Microsoft. Tthey have partnered with Microsoft for logging in (Windows Live ID). However, Microsoft sponsors some of their activities, such as the 2009 U.S. Innovative Teachers Forum, which takes place August 13-14. The theme is "How do you inspire?". I did get a login id and browsed the site: Innovative Teachers Network "...*a global community of educators who share a common interest in enhancing teaching and learning through the innovative use of information and communication technology...*". Interesting site, but very Microsoft-centric.

Also thinking of the future and doing something about it, is the Hamilton-Wentworth District School Board {HWDSB} in Hamilton, Ontario. They host a website and are "...*embarking on a comprehensive review of secondary education with a goal of determining a vision for a secondary education of the future...*".

CH 10 : RELIGION, SEXUALITY AND SEXUAL ORIENTATION

Religion, Sexuality and Sexual orientation

A new bill soon to be passed in the Albert Legislature will require schools to notify parents in advance about subject matter that deals explicitly with religion, sexuality or sexual orientation. Parents have an option to remove their child from such discussions. Some people are a little upset by it, indicating that a public school should be allowed to teach whatever they like and not have to consider the beliefs and teachings of parents. I believe they do have to take parental beliefs into consideration.

Devin Johnson in Manitoba said in a long blog regarding this topic that, "*While it is true that parents can and should play a role in curriculum development, it is equally true that academics, scientists, and educators are uniquely positioned to know what content is most helpful to the intellectual development of students*".
I disagree. That is the old model, which is gone, washed up and laid to rest. The problem is that not all "educators" know it yet.
It is the students who are driving content now. What a concept, eh!
Oh, the basic 3 R's are still there of course but there is a lot of forward thinking taking place now. *Intellectual development* is just one aspect of the whole, which seems to leave out physical development for instance. There are many other influences (mentors, advisors,

leaders, situations, trips, etc) which help a student's *Intellectual development* other than *academics, scientists, and educators.*

I'll get into the "new" content in another blog, but here is a teaser:

paradigm shift

http://members.shaw.ca/priscillatheroux/paradigmshift.html

I laud the government for having the fortitude to go ahead with this bill.

Update:
This statement was made on May 11/09:
"The provincial government has no plans to alter or abandon controversial changes to the Human Rights Act now being considered by MLAs, Culture Minister Lindsay Blackett said Monday."
Update 09/05/15
Culture Minister Lindsay Blackett says he's more sure now than he was two weeks ago that he's doing the right thing by enshrining parental rights in Alberta's Human Rights Act.

CH 10 : COMPUTER GAMES ENHANCE DEXTERITY BUT NOT MENTALITY

Computer games enhance dexterity but not mentality

By mentality, I mean thinking instead of reacting. Computer role playing games, racing games, Rock Band, Guitar Hero, Wii Fit really help those who play develop amazing dexterity and hand-eye coordination. They are faster noticing things, but in my experience seem to be slower focusing on a subject in real life. Multitasking in a game is great, but in real life it is not so easy.

Take a student who is learning to drive. They must know and experience how to steer, break, accelerate, signal, turn and if the vehicle is a standard shift, then they need to know how to use the clutch and shifter. This is not so easy for many students. They also have to check up to two blocks ahead, rear view mirror check, shoulder check and mirror check if turning, watch for kids, stop signs and stop lights, learn how to navigate a traffic circle and much more. A couple of "much more" items are learning how to deal with distractions and learning how to park. They must learn stopping distance based on road conditions, speed, tires, vehicle weight, balance, center of gravity, wide or narrow track, and whether a hard stop is in a straight line or in a turn.

So, not so easy in real life until thinking comes into play.

CH 11 : A TRUTH REVEALED

Parents of Students - a Truth Revealed

To parents of students who have read or heard of Amanda Todd and the many related stories about teenage slip-ups and bullying.

An article which appears in the October 29, 2012 issue of McLean's titled, "Bullied to death" starting on page 68 and written by Emma Teitel, brought up an interesting and very important point.

The article went over some statistics and the author revealed some intimate stories of her own youth.

The point for parents is the last sentence of the article. I quote the words here:
Parents need to understand that for the first time in history, their kids are more likely to get into trouble in the presumed safety of their own homes than they are in the outside world.

Is this already known? Yes - by your children (my child knew) and many parents. Sometimes it is important to state or restate the obvious.

We learn from others and that is our gift.

Good learning..

Update October 26, 2012
A very informal survey of parents leaving a grocery store today revealed that a majority of the parents I

interviewed do monitor their children's internet and mobile phone activities. Very good.

CH 11 : STUDENT YEARS –
SET UP FOR FAILURE?

Student Years - Set Up for Failure?

It seems that many kids from an early age are set up for failure in school. Caring parents hand-hold their kids while going to a park, or store, or school, or pretty well where ever. Kids are dropped off and picked up at kindergarten. Same with grade 1 for most. But most kids haven't learned self-sufficiency or thinking for themselves because their parents do it for them. So the kids spend their first few school years thinking everything will be done for them. Basically we have a dependent generation, and we made them that way. On the other hand we have parents who try to teach their kids to be independent from an early age. They are a small minority. We also have parents, or someone charged with the care of the kids, who don't give the kids the time of day. They just don't care, and after a while neither do the kids. They are a small minority.

Two generations ago kids and parents didn't have to fear kidnapping off the street or have mobile device influence (there were no mobile devices). When in grade one, I took the public bus from grade one up and no one thought anything of it. Nowadays, people would call the parents crazy for letting a five or six year old on a public bus alone. So this is what we've become, paranoid: don't do this, don't do that, watch out for this or that, be careful, yell for help and run, you could hurt yourself, and on and on. What do we have today? Youth gangs, bullies, drug dealers in school, predators - oh wait, are there any good things? Of course, but we don't see those, we concentrate on the negative instead.

Sorry, I digress... Well, what a surprise is in store for kids by junior high school and senior high school. Junior high school isn't too bad. Parents are still doing more than they should but some kids are riding their bikes to school, or taking a public transport bus. Teachers are still helping look after them with some molly-codling here and there. They are getting involved with sports activities and other activities like band, which help broaden their minds. But now it's senior high school. Many kids are already molded. Some are already damaged goods. But for most, there is a rude awakening as no one at school is hand-holding them at all. Heck, nobody cares for the most part. So, many kids go from someone cares to no one cares and this is disheartening to say the least. Some kids form small like-minded groups and become "friends". Some stay loners. Some say "get me outa here!" and some say "but I don't want to grow up". Aging, whether growing up or not, is not an option a student can escape from. Well, there is one way, suicide. And some do take that option. But for most it becomes a reality, accepted or not. How did school help the student become an educated, happy adult? *(Well, even though this started as a rhetorical question, there is an answer. Teachers look good if their students look good, as in do well and be happy with their learning. So, most teachers "care" while school is in. But there is no time afterwards. Teachers also have a life.)*
So even though the student graduated, or not, how do

they feel? Do they feel accomplished, knowledgeable, confident, caring, happy - or not? And if not, why not? To me, regardless of the answer to "why not", failure in the mind is the result. Perhaps dependency is a key.

So, an adult now. Wow. You mean I have to "work"! What! Ok, for a few, drugs seem to be the escapist answer. But you need money for drugs. Hmmm, I know, steal it from someone else who works to have a life style they like. How did the kids/adults get here (in this state)? Well, I think parents and certain peers had a lot to do with it. Monkey see, monkey do. So we're still working the "educated, happy adult".

For the most part, adult kids seem to be ok. Responsibility seems to take longer to assume. Thought out decision-making seems to take longer, as there are not enough life experiences yet. Now, we are talking about students in North America, Canada, and Alberta - not the rest of the world. Life experience and "growing up" happens very quickly - pre-teen and teen - in some other countries in the world.

So, how many fail? Well, the survey says - wait, what survey? The one where a percentage were polled with fixed leading questions and the paperwork was sent in or the poll was done online. Some poll. And, some people actually believe the results. Ok, we don't have figures. A "large number" of grade 12 grads go to college or university. Another "large number" do not. What does "large number" mean to you?

The ones who do not immediately go to college or

university after grade 12 graduation are now gaining more life experience related to work, play, other persons of interest, career choices, travel, exploration, self-development, preparing for the new world and so on.

Those who do go on to formal education opportunities have more to look forward to in the future perhaps, but living for the future is not always consistent with living life as it is today.

Ok, I did digress again. In summary, we have to let the kids have more responsibility by letting go a bit earlier than we would like. Some kids have already experienced "life" because their parents don't care about them or what they do, at all. The majority of kids do have caring home lives though. These kids need an education which is gentle but thorough - what is "out there" which can impact them in a negative way if they are let loose but just "don't know". Some parents educate their kids. Some do not. Some want to protect their kids to adulthood. Unless the kids are locked up at home, it can't be done.

Kids need to learn and experience. Hopefully the learning from parents comes first.

Really though, how did schooling help the student become an educated, happy adult? Or was the student set up for failure right from grade one?

Yes I could keep going, but I'll stop now.

Learn what you enjoy - enjoy what you learn...

CH 11 : HOMEWORK – IS IT STILL NECESSARY?

Homework - is it still necessary?

Homework has been the bane of their existence for students everywhere. But is it necessary?

Here is School Library Journal talking with Alfie Kohn. *"Why do schools keep giving more homework when research shows there's no correlation to academic achievement?..."*

I found this statement by a commenter at For and Against,

http://www.forandagainst.com/Homework_Is_Necessary

"...Homework is schoolwork to take home, because the school day isn't long enough for the teachers to make sure that the students are fully and correctly learned in the days lesson...".
Now if that indeed is the case, then change the teaching model, the lesson plan or the teacher.

More on the subject of homework (and new math) is at IS HOMEWORK NECESSARY?.

http://www.gothamgazette.com/article/education/200609 26/6/1983

On the other hand, Is Homework Necessary and How do I Grade It?.

http://successfulteaching.blogspot.com/2008/04/is-homework-necessary-and-how-do-i.html

And on the other hand, Homework robs children of their childhood.

http://www.theage.com.au/articles/2004/05/20/10850284 63584.html

There is much more about this topic but this blog illustrates the issue.

CH 11 : MORE ON HOMEWORK AND PARENT/STUDENT STRESS

More on Homework and Parent/Student Stress

In a previous article I talked about homework stress.

http://www.privsec.com/blogs/blog5.php/2009/10/30/majority-of-parents-find-homework-stress

Here is another article which tells the story of a Calgary family that signed a no homework agreement with the Calgary School Board.

Here is a quote from the article linked below, "*Tom Milley was frustrated by the amount of homework given to his children.*
A Calgary family caught between busy careers, hectic school schedules and extracurricular activities has sought relief by signing a contract with their school to ban homework."
For those who are not lawyers, here is a good balanced article from Anna-Liza Kozma, a writer with the CBC. A quote, "*Childhood passes quickly. And so do sunny days.*
That means, in our house, sunshine trumps homework pretty much every time."

Here is the link to Negotiating an end to the homework debate.
http://www.cbc.ca/canada/story/2009/11/24/f-vp-kozma.html

Good teaching...Good listening...

CH 11 : MAJORITY OF PARENTS FIND HOMEWORK STRESSFUL

Majority of parents find homework Stressful

From the CBC comes this article today about a national survey result released Monday.

It is titled, "Majority of parents find homework Stressful", and discusses an Edmonton teacher's response. The study was commissioned by the Canadian Council on Learning.

Jackie Pocklington, a teacher at a grade school in Edmonton, refuses to hand out homework.

Visit the article linked above to see why.

Good Teaching... Good Learning...

CH 11 : TALKING WITH KIDS ABOUT SCHOOL

Talking with Kids about School

I found a great resource about talking with kids about school. It is from PBS. The four web page article includes; Understanding Each Other, Talking Strategies, Questions that Work and Age and Stage Tips.

There is a lot more for parents at the site as well, just check the sidebar.

Here is an excerpt from the introduction page, *"Why is it so hard to talk about school? Parents often get exasperated with kids' monosyllabic answers to their simple questions. That one well-intentioned line, "How was school today?" has probably provoked more bad feelings between parents and kids than either party ever intended."*

There is some really good advice and very workable changes for parents on this topic. So, please have a look at the intro page called, Talking with Kids about School, to get started.

http://www.pbs.org/parents/goingtoschool/talk_child.html

How many parents have had the conversation illustrated in the cartoon on the page? I know as a parent I have, which is why I found this site so interesting and the straight examples so good. I consider the site a valuable resource for parents.

That's all for now...

CH 11 : KIDS AND EXPERIENCE

Kids and Experience

Today we look at kids and experience. What kind of experience? Well, getting over shyness, going back to school and more.

Parental experience is next. Parents have to be ready for school, in order to help their children be ready for school. Here is a helpful article called, Parents: Start the School Year Off on the Right Foot, which may help both parents and students together.

http://backtoschool.about.com/od/forparents/Parents_Start_the_School_Year_Off_on_the_Right_Foot.htm

"Study: Game experiences can provide hands-on learning opportunities" By Kristin Kalning. It is called, Can games make your kid a better citizen?

http://www.msnbc.msn.com/id/26726230/

Here is a consideration which isn't usually thought of, as it is outside the experience of most people. The education experience of military children. Here is a US DoD article which helps explain it better than I can. It is called, Ensuring Kids get Quality, Consistent Education.

http://www.defenselink.mil/news/newsarticle.aspx?id=44765

A quote from the article, "*In some of our small and remote locations we need to ensure the kids are getting the same kind of qualities and 'the comprehensive high school experience' that they are getting in our larger schools*".

There are summer camps, road trips, overseas trips, ski trips and more, all designed to give kids an experience they haven't had before. Here is one long term experience that most haven't heard of doing. What kids can do - Yupik Eskimo Youth Embrace Subsistence Living and Renew Community.

http://www.whatkidscando.org/specialcollections/student_research_action/russian mission/index.html

Experience counts! Programs such as Venturers or Civil Air Patrol are great confidence builders as well as gaining life experience.

CH 11 : THE PARADOX OF THE ANXIOUS PARENT

The Paradox of the Anxious Parent

To throw a monkey wrench into our school/teacher/parent thinking, this is the article to read!

The Paradox of the Anxious Parent by Dr. Michael Thompson, Ph.D.

http://publiusrex.wordpress.com/2009/02/27/the-paradox-of-the-anxious-parent-dr-michael-thompson-phd/

There isn't anything more I can say today...

CH 12 : TEACHERS – JUDGE, JURY AND EXECUTIONER

Teachers - Judge, Jury and Executioner

Are teachers in our grade school system still acting as Judge, Jury and Executioner?

Well, to have any order in the classroom, it would seem to be so. However, like any quasi-judicial system, there are good decisions and decisions which would require appeal. Some decisions are not well thought out. There is an appeal procedure in place, right?

Some teachers are not particularly well trained in the art of classroom discipline apparently. Teachers have to know the law, school board guidelines, which are like laws, and local school policies, which are like laws.

Classroom discipline entails questions and eye contact, listening, engagement, decision-making (not off-the-cuff decision-making, but informed decision-making) and much more.

I am reminded of a recent (last few days) decision by a teacher. The teacher was supervising a final quiz before exams. Some students finished early but were not allowed to leave. Some kids were talking quietly at the back of the classroom. The teacher came up to the first boy closest to him and accused him of talking while the quiz was in progress. The boy said "I wasn't talking". The teacher said, "You're a liar. Give me your paper." He tore the paper in half and said to the boy that it will be marked as a zero. The boy walked out. Interesting that the boy who was talking at the time was sitting behind the accused and didn't say a thing. He let the innocent boy be tarred and feathered and lose his quiz mark, and he didn't say a thing. I think he must be a coward, or has no integrity at all.

For this particular teacher, it was his last year after a long teaching career. So, there is probably no appeal because classes are finished and exams are being written and the teacher is now retired. Great eh!

So now we know how some students get into the "don't care" mindset. And the teacher? Well, I would have to say teachers are still Judge, Jury and Executioner, without reprieve or appeal or perhaps reason. For some, just an off day perhaps.

From the tone of this blog entry you may read between the lines that I am not too happy with the situation. I'm not happy because I know the accused boy, I know he is not lying, and I know the teacher didn't take it any further than the first boy he came into contact with.

Fortunately this was grade 11 and not grade 12. There will have to be something in place for grade 12. Perhaps much more thoughtful meet the teacher discussions to start.

Students: if you think it won't matter in 20 years then perhaps don't worry about it, as in don't lose sleep over it. When it comes to relationships though, quite often a person will still remember it 20 years later. If you think the effects, etc. will still matter in 20 years, than do something about it, now.

Good learning - I hope...

CH 12 : STUDENT OR TEACHER –
PROVE ME RIGHT

Student or Teacher - Prove Me Right

Have you ever sat in class and knowing the teacher made a mistake, wanted to correct her? Well, nowadays the students can do so.

Here is an example. The teacher is teaching a subject related to Chemistry, but it is not in her knowledge base. Chemistry is. However, she studied to come up to speed, came to class and met her students for the first time. It didn't take long for the students to realize she didn't know her subject too well, although they could see she was trying her best. So, now it is almost the end of the school year and she is still trying and also knows her students better, like the few who sleep through her class but always seem to know the subject and easily pass the quizzes and exams and the ones who appear to have a glazed look most of the time.

So, the students came up with an idea as to how they can learn the right answers and help the teacher at the same time. The students, using their iPhone or Android mobile devices, Google what she says and compare it to search-related subject matter appearing on legitimate, recognized websites. If what the teacher is saying is wrong, a student will correct her. Wow! Everyone learns!

If I had this class, I would bring in a cooler of Popsicles

and offer one to any student who could prove me wrong, and why, about whatever I said related to the subject at hand during the class. Heck, I would deliberately get something wrong just so a student would win a Popsicle. I probably wouldn't have to make it deliberate though.:) I think the listening and learning would be phenomenal. Ok, perhaps that's just me, but I would hope others share the same idea.

Mobile devices are not going away, so let's use them to the best of our, and our students, ability.

"Better education - electronically!"
No, we still need the human touch. Story-telling to illustrate a point or emphasizing a particular component, answering a critical question, or re-stating a concept because eye contact indicates not everyone is comprehending what was said. I believe the list of reasons could go on for a long time and fill many pages. However, teachers can use school and student technology to help them "get the message across" and insure learning takes place.

Remember: *As Sonny Malone (Michael Beck) said to his boss in a movie,* "Tuesday is Wednesday" - until the end of high school.

Good learning...Good understanding...

CH 12 : BRING IT ON – CHANGE IN THOUGHT IN EDUCATION

Bring it on - Change in Thought in Education

Well, as usual, Sir Ken Robinson has stirred the pot again.

This time he is saying, "Bring on the learning revolution".

http://www.ted.com/talks/sir_ken_robinson_bring_on_the_revolution.html

This is a May 2010 TED talk and here is an excerpt from the TED webpage describing the talk: "*In this poignant, funny follow-up to his fabled 2006 talk, Sir Ken Robinson makes the case for a radical shift from standardized schools to personalized learning—creating conditions where kids' natural talents can flourish.*".

His previous talk, "schools kill creativity", is linked on the talk page.

Good teaching...

CH 12 : TEACHERS AS MEDIATORS

Teachers as Mediators

Teachers as Mediators - "Mediators" means different things to different people. What is meant here is the teacher as a mediator between curriculum policy and implementation. As well, we will discuss teachers as a different kind of "mediator", really a Critical Incident Stress (CIS) debriefer. We'll also talk about conflict mediators.

We will start with this paper called, School reactivation programs after disaster: could teachers serve as clinical mediators?

http://bases.bireme.br/cgi-bin/wxislind.exe/iah/online/?IsisScript=iah/iah.xis&src=google&base=ADOLEC&lang=p&nextAction=lnk&exprSearch=12725016&indexSearch=ID

A quote from the summary, "*The tremendous needs that emerge after a disaster and the reluctance shown by most victims to seek professional help require mental health leaders to adopt a proactive stance and implement relief programs in the child's most natural setting. The school as institution and the teachers as empowered mediators offer the appropriate conditions for implementing an effective large-scale intervention program.*". Empowering teachers means training in Critical Incident Stress debriefing techniques. Not everyone is good at it and the initial course is usually two days. However, the CIS debriefer can literally save a life.

This one, the teacher as a mediator between curriculum policy and implementation, is the toughest one to research.

This one is especially good and the link to the abstract, and download, is called, Teachers as critical mediators of knowledge.

http://hub.hku.hk/handle/123456789/54294

This link looks at the school as a policy mediator. It is called, Implementing Nunavut Education Act: Compulsory School Attendance Policy.

http://www.umanitoba.ca/publications/cjeap/articles/kwarteng_nunavut.html

CH 12 : STUDENTS AND TECHNOLOGY AND TEACHERS

Students and Technology and Teachers

Some teachers and schools refuse to acknowledge the fact that kids today have, and use, modern technology. Technology that many parents depend on. For example, parents texting their child to inform him/her of something important. Or a child texting a parent regarding an important message. This messaging normally takes place on their phones.

Now here is the problem: teachers either taking their phones or giving the student grief for receiving or replying to a message. Yes, it could be just a message from a friend, but what if it isn't? In some cases the phone is a lifeline. Most of the time, the phone use isn't even in the classroom. And of course, the teacher should not be taking the phone in the first place.

In my opinion, teachers should not hassle students for using modern technology. The students of my acquaintance are very considerate when using their phones. And, the phones are no longer just expensive toys. The phones are important tools to use, which includes the lifeline function.

Sooner or later schools/teachers will have to recognize that the world is changing. Give the kids a break. Ok, some kids will take advantage of a more liberal phone policy, but they can be handled on an individual basis.

Dr. Mike

ABOUT THE AUTHOR

DrMike@privsec.com

Among other things, Dr. Mike (Michael) is an Author and Teacher.

He is involved with many aspects of education today and over the last thirty-five years. He is an instructor, educator, teacher, trainer, lecturer and public speaker. He provides classroom and field instruction on a variety of topics such as, How to speak and be heard, Lesson planning, Projecting your voice, Public speaker training, How to address diverse audiences, Talking to young audiences, Interviewing and Investigation and much more.

He is not a psychologist or psychiatrist, just a man with a lot of insight and, he believes, common sense. He is concerned, and this book is a reflection of his learning, education and mostly, experience. This is one person's story.

Because of his background, the author conducts/moderates student/parent crisis interventions on occasion. The author is also involved in a program called "Getting it Back", which help students regain their self-esteem (self-confidence) as a bully-proofing measure.

He has an education blog for students and teachers in the 21st century. This blog covers many aspects of schooling such as, critical thinking, homework, depression, suicide, recovery, bullying, forward thinking and planning, how do you inspire, parental rights and much more. The blog is the source for this book.

He was an Emergency Planning Officer with a provincial government. His experience also includes Ground Search and Rescue in all capacities for over 30 years; Canadian Coast Guard Auxiliary for 15 years, 10 operational, and 6 as coxswain; and Air spotter for 3 years.

He started, organized and built a non-profit organization beginning in 1983. It eventually had 4 employees and about 55 volunteer members.

He helped get a wilderness child survival program called, Lost in the Woods, off the ground, starting in 1984.

He developed an Interview and Investigations course for special services. That is where the emphasis on "listening" was developed.

There was a need for Critical Incident Stress (CIS) debriefings for several years, so he became qualified as a CIS debriefer to help his colleagues. He developed a network of debriefers and one psychologist (for insight and help).

He built his first web site in 1995 and featured help articles regarding youth enduring critical disaster mental health issues, responses and help, which were written by a professional working for the federal government at the time.

His interest in helping others to get back on an even keel after a very disturbing experience has been ongoing for over 30 years.

He was also involved as an Advisor for a Venture group for 3 years.

He was involved in many crime scene searches over the years.

He was involved as an extra in a TV series.

He was a paraglider and an ultralight pilot.

He has been involved in many, many things over the years, all of which make him what he is today. A person with huge experience and knowledge with insight that can zero in to the real personal issues.

He doesn't have all the answers. However in many cases, he can help you find your answer or path.

In memory of Jamie Hubley, who said this before he died, "*You cant break. . . When you're already broken.*".

However I believe you can be helped and "repaired", like a broken bone. Help those who want to help you, help you.

Disclaimer:

There are no guarantees in life. Most of what you read here is from personal experience or knowledge. Some of the experiences were gained without asking and with much mental anguish. Please consider these entries (typos included) as stories that help illustrate a point of view. You are responsible for you. No one else is. If you try something you learned from reading this book. Great, you tried - feel good! If it didn't work for you, then try something else or a variation. Don't blame the author for just trying to help by sharing. There are no diagnoses per se here, just blunt, honest truth as the author sees it - after a lifetime of seeing, knowing, caring, experiencing and living it.

This is not a self-help book. It is a book of experience and insight. The author hopes something you read here will resonate with you and therefore help you in a very positive way. We want to keep you in the here and now, and alive and well again. There is no telling what impact you will make as you live, only time will tell. Let's try - and make a difference! You may be the key - for positive outcomes for many other people. By example perhaps?

Photos are by Michael.

Dr. Mike

Index